The *Right* Words

Also by Wynton C. Hall

*Home of the Brave: Honoring the Unsung Heroes in the
War on Terror* (coauthor Caspar W. Weinberger)

*The Greatest Communicator: What Ronald Reagan
Taught Me about Politics, Leadership, and Life*
(coauthor Dick Wirthlin)

The *Right* Words

Great Republican Speeches
That Shaped History

Wynton C. Hall

John Wiley & Sons, Inc.

Published by John Wiley & Sons, Inc., Hoboken, New Jersey
Published simultaneously in Canada

Design and composition by Navta Associates, Inc.

For general information about our other products and services, please contact our Customer Care Department within the United States at (800) 762-2974, outside the United States at (317) 572-3993 or fax (317) 572-4002.

Wiley also publishes its books in a variety of electronic formats. Some content that appears in print may not be available in electronic books. For more information about Wiley products, visit our web site at www.wiley.com.

Library of Congress Cataloging-in-Publication Data:

Hall, Wynton C., date.
   The right words : great Republican speeches that shaped history / Wynton C. Hall.
      p. cm.
   Includes index.
   ISBN 978-0-471-75816-7 (cloth)
1. United States—Politics and government—Sources. 2. Speeches, addresses, etc., American.
3. Republican Party (U.S. : 1854-)—History—Sources. I. Title.
E183.H29 2007
973.09'9—dc22

                                                                                        2006021033

Printed in the United States of America

10 9 8 7 6 5 4 3 2 1

For Kate

We regard speaking well to be the clearest sign of a good mind, which it requires, and truthful, lawful, and just speech we consider the image of a good and faithful soul.

—Isocrates, *Nicocles* 3.7

CONTENTS

CONTENTS

CONTENTS

ACKNOWLEDGMENTS

Speeches don't write themselves. Neither do books. Both represent the collective efforts of a cast of many who remain hidden from their audiences. Several individuals assisted with this book, each of whom I wish to thank.

Whatever I know about rhetoric I owe to my graduate school mentor and friend, Baylor University Distinguished Professor of Rhetoric and Communication Dr. Martin J. Medhurst, formerly of Texas A&M University. Marty's passion for rhetoric became my own. I thank him for his support through the years and, most of all, for his friendship.

I've had the great fortune of writing books with two of my political mentors: Ronald Reagan's chief political strategist and pollster Dick Wirthlin and Reagan's secretary of defense Caspar W. Weinberger. Dick taught me that politics and integrity are not mutually exclusive. He remains one of the most respected presidential strategists in history for a reason. I also want to thank Cap Weinberger. Cap passed away during the writing of this book. He was at once courtly and humble, and he had a way about him that won you over instantly. Cap and Dick were of the "old school" in politics that believed a person could fight for his beliefs and still maintain comity and decorum. I pray we can bring some of that back.

I express my appreciation for my friend former Reagan and George H. W. Bush press secretary Marlin Fitzwater, one of the most humble, humorous, cigar-smoking men I know, and the consummate communications professional to boot. I also wish to thank Reagan speechwriters Tony Dolan, Peter Robinson, and Peggy Noonan; Gerald R. Ford speechwriter Craig R. Smith; George H. W. Bush speechwriter Curt Smith; and George W. Bush speechwriters Marc Thiessen and Michael Gerson. Through the granting of interviews and the words you've wrought, you have proven that the right words don't just materialize; they are crafted, often under difficult and tense circumstances. Thank you for serving your presidents and your nation with your gifts.

My gratitude also goes to those who provided research support, including Yale University, George H. W. Bush Presidential Library; Bainbridge College; Young America's Foundation; the Republican National Committee; and the Everett Dirksen Center.

My gratitude extends to the Hoover Institution at Stanford University. Special thanks go to Hoover president Dr. John Raisian for appointing me as a visiting fellow and to senior associate director Richard Sousa for his continued support.

I am grateful for John Wiley & Sons and publisher Kitt Allan, as well as senior production editor Lisa Burstiner and freelance copy editor Steven M. Long. I am especially thankful for senior editor Hana Lane. Hana's gifts are myriad. She possesses an encyclopedic knowledge of, well, just about anything historical. But Hana's greatest talent is her ability to spur you to approach a passage from a crisp, fresh angle you might not have otherwise seen. She is, quite simply, a delight.

Joe Vallely, my literary agent, is one of the best in the business. His indefatigable support and ironclad friendship are, as ever, appreciated.

To my friends who supported me through the writing of this book, I offer my deepest thanks: Peter and Rochelle Schweizer, Yusuf and Nicole Haidermota, Phil Reyes, Jack Weisser, Scott and Amanda Renick, Scott and Carey Watts, Stan and Jenna Miley, Tim and Shelly Matthews, Paul Kengor, and Tim Watkins.

My family remains my rock. Dad, Mom, Bill, Gretchen, Holly, Leslie, Creighton, and Jane—your love and support humble me. Most of all, I want my beautiful bride and best friend, Katie, and our angel, Bella Kate, to know how much their patience and love mean to me. You inspire me daily. Thank you.

The author alone is responsible for the contents of this book.

The Elephant Poachers

*Leftist Academe and the Erasure
of Republican Remembrance*

*The first step in liquidating a people is to erase its memory.
Destroy its books, its culture, its history. Then have somebody write
new books, manufacture a new culture, invent a new history. Before
long the nation will begin to forget what it is and what it was.*
—Milan Kundera

This book is based on a simple if profound truth: *words matter.*

Sometimes this axiom is self-evident. While reading the words of an old love letter or poem, for example, a phrase or a line can be so dazzling, so powerful that it almost seems to levitate off the printed page, like a magician's assistant rising and hovering in midair. The line sparkles with significance, and we instantly sense its importance.

At other times, however, it is not until several months or years after we've read or heard something that we begin to grasp how consequential the words turned out to be. With the benefit of hindsight and history on our side, we come to appreciate the gravity of the words and their effect. Yet everywhere and always we find that, indeed, words matter.

Though intangible, words create real change. They possess the power to alter the contours of history, especially in a democracy. Words can make financial markets soar and crash, pardon the imprisoned, bring solace to a mourning nation, and begin and end wars. Words, it turns out, are the axis on which human events spin.

This is a book about those words—the *right* words—that shaped history. More specifically, this is a book about Republican speeches that mattered. Why *Republican* speeches? Because they more than their Democratic counterparts are given short shrift by the keeper of the national consciousness: academia. Leftist professors work vigorously to ignore, undermine, and dismiss Republican words and deeds. This is not part of some conspiracy, mind you. Rather, it is the predictable result of a radicalized professoriate that rejects the legitimacy and import of words that emanate from orators right of center. And whether citizens realize it or not, the scope of the problem is far worse—and longer-lasting—than many have assumed.

First, there is the challenge posed by the ideological meat grinders that are our nation's universities. It's no secret that liberal professors and administrators dominate today's collegiate landscape. But in 2005, veteran *Washington Post* reporter Howard Kurtz warned that the matter was far worse than many had assumed: "College faculties, long assumed to be a liberal bastion, lean further to the left than even the most conspiratorial conservatives might have imagined." Kurtz then went on to cite a study by Robert Lichter of George Mason University and fellow political science professors Stanley Rothman of Smith College and Neil Nevitte of the University of Toronto that found that 72 percent of those teaching at American universities and colleges are liberal and 15 percent are conservative. Moreover, while 50 percent of the faculty members surveyed identified themselves as Democrats, only 11 percent were Republicans. The divide only widened at elite colleges and universities. There, 87 percent of the faculty was liberal and only 13 percent conservative. It seems that the liberal love affair with diversity does not include *intellectual* diversity. This imbalance has prompted some state legislatures to begin considering whether efforts should be made to ensure that public universities offer students a truly balanced education.[1]

Many university professors' far-left ideology places them outside mainstream opinion on a host of issues. As Kurtz writes, many professors are "to the left of the Democratic Party."[2] To wit: University of Colorado professor Ward Churchill's disgraceful statement that the men, women, and children murdered in the World Trade Center during the September 11 terrorist attacks were nothing more than "little Eichmanns" (a reference to Adolf Eichmann, the man Adolf Hitler tasked with annihilating millions of Jews during the Holocaust). Churchill is not alone; there are scores of far-left professors.[3] Yet Churchill's outrageous comments were not only deeply offensive and painful to both Jews and the families of 9/11 victims, but they also served as a wake-up call to the deterioration of the modern academy.

So why do liberal Democrats dominate our nation's campuses? It is reasonable to ask whether the partisan and ideological imbalance in most faculties is the fault of conservatives and Republicans. After all, Republicans are free to get their master's and doctoral degrees and apply for these positions. So why don't they?

That's easy to explain, says George Lakoff, linguistics professor at Berkeley and top Democratic communications strategist. "Unlike conservatives, [Democrats] believe in working for the public good and social justice, as well as knowledge and art for their own sake, which are what the humanities and social sciences are about."[4] Matching such smugness and hyperelitism is difficult. But Duke University philosophy chairman Robert Brandon managed to outdo Lakoff when he explained to the *Chronicle of Higher Education* that there was no ideological bias in academic hiring. Dr. Brandon said that the gross disparities between Republican and Democratic professors were perfectly logical: "We try to hire the best, smartest people available. If, as John Stuart Mill said, stupid people are generally conservative, then there are lots of conservatives we will never hire. Mill's analysis may go some way towards explaining the power of the Republican Party in our society and the relative scarcity of Republicans in academia."[5]

With professors like Dr. Brandon holding major university chair positions, it is little wonder that hundreds of students across the nation continue to report ideological harassment and discrimination from leftist professors. Groups like the Foundation for Individual Rights in

Education, Campus Watch, and Young America's Foundation have formed in response to the liberal bias many conservative students experience. But even with these efforts, many Republicans are not sanguine about the prospects for change. Emory University English professor Mark Bauerlein says that leftist ideology has become so deeply entrenched in universities today that it has redefined entire fields of study, thus eliminating conservative professors from consideration:

> Schools of education, for instance, take constructivist theories of learning as definitive, excluding realists (in matters of knowledge) on principle, while the quasi-Marxist outlook of cultural studies rules out those who espouse capitalism. If you disapprove of affirmative action, forget pursuing a degree in African-American studies. If you think that the nuclear family proves the best unit of social well-being, stay away from women's studies.[6]

In this way, Bauerlein explains, conservatives are automatically nullified from consideration for academic positions, hardly a troubling development for the leftist-dominated academy. After all, the thinking goes, why teach and present respectfully that which you don't respect? The result, therefore, is that students receive a lopsided education; the ideological snobbery and partisan chicanery rolls on.

Equally troubling is what such intellectual snobbery means for the presentation of history, especially American history, on college campuses. That's assuming, of course, students are even *taught* American history. As early as 1988, the National Endowment for the Humanities sounded the alarms when it reported that more than 80 percent of colleges and universities permitted students to graduate without taking a course in American history. By 2002, 100 percent of the country's top colleges and universities required not a single class in American history to graduate. To satisfy history requirements, students may instead take courses such as "Alternative Sexual Identities and Communities" and "No Body's Perfect."

A central goal of the Marxist ideology to which many leftist professors subscribe involves the deconstruction of history by exploring the "marginalized voices" who have suffered under "American oppression." For this to succeed, history must be taught in such a way as to focus on the evils of America's past while ignoring or mitigating its virtues. So far it seems to be working. In 2000, the American Council of Trustees and Alumni commissioned the independent Roper polling organization to survey college seniors at America's top fifty-five colleges and universities (as reported by *U.S. News & World Report*) to determine their level of historical literacy. The results were alarming: just 38 percent of college seniors knew the significance of Valley Forge; a paltry 23 percent could identify James Madison as the "Father of the Constitution"; and only 22 percent of college seniors were able to identify "Government of the people, by the people, for the people" as a line from Abraham Lincoln's Gettysburg Address—the most famous presidential speech in American history. The only history safe from extinction belonged to MTV: A full 98 percent of college seniors were able to identify rapper Snoop Dogg, while 99 percent could identify the cartoon characters Beavis and Butthead.

Besides the elimination of American history, the staggering number of liberal professors on college campuses has created a learning environment that many students say has morphed into indoctrination. In 2005, the American Council of Trustees again wanted to survey college seniors at America's top fifty colleges and universities (as reported by *U.S. News & World Report*). This time they had the Center for Research and Analysis at the University of Connecticut conduct a survey to determine how, if at all, professors' ideologies or political leanings influenced the way students were taught. The results are disturbing:

- 47 percent of students reported that their professors made negative comments about conservatives. Only 15 percent said professors made negative comments about liberals.
- 29 percent of students said they felt that they had to agree with a professor's political views to get a good grade.

- 42 percent of students felt that course readings were one-sided.

- 68 percent of students reported that their professors made negative comments about President George W. Bush. Only 17 percent said professors made negative comments about Senator John Kerry. Instead, 62 percent of students said their professors made positive comments about Senator Kerry.[7]

Taken together, all of these factors—faculties overwhelmingly composed of leftist Democrats, partisan faculty hiring, the elimination of American history courses, and slanted course readings and lectures filled with liberal bias—suggest that our nation's college students are receiving a biased view of Republican contributions to history.

For these reasons and others, many Americans suffer from an acute form of "Republican historical amnesia." By showcasing some of the most significant moments of Republican oratory, this book is meant to serve as a corrective against the "elephant poachers"—leftist academics who wish to raze Republican contributions.

Partisanship manifests itself in policy positions as well as in prose. As we will see, Republican rhetoric contains at least three common denominators. The first is an unwavering celebration of individualism, the idea that individuals are responsible for their failures and successes, and that each person represents an autonomous will capable of moral choice making and self-advancement. Republican oratory, therefore, tends to demonstrate an unflinching rejection of collectivism.

Second, from Lincoln to George W. Bush, Judeo-Christian themes, allusions, and imagery have filled Republican speeches. For a time, the same could be said of Democratic oratory. But no more. William F. Buckley Jr. once said that it was possible but not likely for a conservative to be an atheist, Ayn Rand, one supposes, being the closest approximation. To be sure, it is important to note that there is a difference between being a Republican and being a conservative. But since conservatives are chief among Republican ranks, GOP oratory continues to sound themes that resonate with Judeo-Christian values and beliefs.

Finally, the Republican Party has long stood for a strong national defense. Civil liberties are hard to exercise if one is dead; Republicans believe that security is the wellspring from which liberty flows. Thus, Republican speeches have often bulged with a military muscularity that has no compunction about the use of lethal force to defend life and liberty. The same cannot be said for Democratic speakers, many of whose orations bend toward pacifism, antimilitarism, and the rejection of force as a catalyst for personal and national liberty and freedom.

To be sure, many of the words spoken by America's Republican presidents and party leaders have been forgotten with little harm to the Republic. But some words must *never* be forgotten.

After all, what would the nation look like today had Abraham Lincoln's second inaugural address argued for regional retribution instead of national healing? Where might America be today had Dwight D. Eisenhower remained silent on September 24, 1957, instead of standing on the side of nine black students who were denied access to Little Rock's Central High School? What would the plight of African Americans be today without the courage and determination of Senator Everett Dirksen standing up and making the Civil Rights Act of 1964 possible? Where would the American conservative movement, which did not exist before 1945, be today without its first presidential candidate, Barry Goldwater, and one of its most eloquent spokesmen, William F. Buckley Jr.? Fast forward to the 1980s and ask yourself: Is it even possible to think about the fall of the Soviet Union and the Berlin Wall without seeing Ronald Reagan standing at the Brandenburg Gate thundering for all the world to hear, "Mr. Gorbachev, tear down this wall!"? And finally, would the historic elections in Afghanistan and Iraq have occurred absent George W. Bush rallying Americans to meet "Our mission and our moment" as he did on September 20, 2001?

Regardless of partisanship, Americans must understand that these words shaped the contours of human history. These words mattered. A people that forgets its past condemns its future. It ambles. It loses

1

Abraham Lincoln

The First and Greatest

The Gettysburg Address

NOVEMBER 19, 1863

BATTLEFIELD, GETTYSBURG, PENNSYLVANIA

It is a flat failure.

—Abraham Lincoln to his friend Ward
Lamon after delivering the Gettysburg Address

Four score and seven years ago our fathers brought forth on this continent a new nation, conceived in Liberty, and dedicated to the proposition that all men are created equal.

Now we are engaged in a great civil war, testing whether that nation or any nation so conceived and so dedicated, can long endure. We are met on a great battle-field of that war. We have come to dedicate a portion of that field, as a final resting place for those who here gave their lives that that nation might live. It is altogether fitting and proper that we should do this.

But, in a larger sense, we can not dedicate—we can not consecrate—we can not hallow—this ground. The brave men, living and dead, who struggled here, have consecrated it, far above our poor power to add or detract. The world will little note, nor long remember what we say here, but it can never forget what they did here. It is for us the living, rather, to be dedicated here to the unfinished work which they who fought here have thus far so nobly advanced. It is rather for us to be here dedicated to the great task remaining before us—that from these honored dead we take increased devotion to that cause for which they gave the last full measure of devotion—that we here highly resolve that these dead shall not have died in vain—that this nation, under God, shall have a new birth of freedom—and that government of the people, by the people, for the people, shall not perish from the earth.

Throughout his life, Abraham Lincoln was surrounded by death. He was born on February 12, 1809, in a log cabin on a Kentucky farm, and his childhood and early adulthood had been an arduous lesson in mortality. His younger brother, Thomas, died in infancy. Then, when Abraham was nine years old, his mother, Nancy Lincoln, contracted "milk sickness" from her uncle and aunt, Thomas and Elizabeth Sparrow. The disease was caused by drinking milk from cows that had ingested poisonous white snakeroot. That all three individuals had fallen ill was doubly difficult for Lincoln, as the Sparrows had been like grandparents to him. So when Thomas and Elizabeth died from milk sickness, Lincoln was crestfallen. But his grief would pale to that which he would experience two weeks later when Nancy succumbed to the disease as well. On her deathbed, just moments before her final passing, Lincoln's mother told him, "I am going away from you, Abraham. And I shall not return."[1]

Ten years later, at the age of nineteen, Lincoln's older sister, Sarah, died while giving birth. Following Nancy's passing, Sarah had been like a second mother to Lincoln. Yet again, Lincoln had been forced to absorb loss, and with it the melancholy that would hover over him like a fog throughout his life. Even as he delivered the speech for which he is most remembered—the Gettysburg Address—Lincoln had donned the symbols of death. His iconic black silk stovepipe hat had been outfitted with a mourner's ribbon to recognize the recent death of yet another person close to him: his beloved son Willie. He had *worn* death.

Indeed, Lincoln felt at home with loss. He had numbed himself to its pain. And so perhaps it should not be surprising that as president Lincoln delivered his most famous speech while standing inside the vortex of a war that had become a whirlwind of human carnage. The pangs of loss Lincoln had experienced throughout his life had burrowed themselves into the rhythms and cadence of his rhetoric. And it was these qualities that culminated on November 19, 1863, in the greatest presidential speech in U.S. history.

It is hard for modern people to wrap their minds around the magnitude of death the Civil War produced. Two percent of the entire U.S. population had been killed, roughly 618,000 dead. Were such losses to be experienced given today's U.S. population, they would result in roughly six million dead Americans. What's more, over the course of those four blood-soaked years, it was quite common for two- and three-day battles to account for more deaths than the total loss experienced in some U.S. wars. From July 1–3, 1863, the three-day Battle of Gettysburg claimed fifty thousand men, almost as many men as would die during the eleven years of U.S. involvement in the Vietnam War.

To be sure, during the 1800s death was a much more prevalent and accepted part of daily life. Infant mortality rates and deaths from diseases and childbirth were exponentially higher than those of the twentieth and twenty-first centuries. Likely because of this fact, people living in the nineteenth century possessed a fascination with death in general and cemeteries in particular. Historian Garry Wills goes so far as to describe the period as a "culture of death." And it is in this context that Lincoln's Gettysburg Address must be viewed.[2]

Yet even given the more accepted attitudes toward human loss, the Battle of Gettysburg had been especially brutal, even by Civil War standards. The three-day summer battle began on the morning of July 1, when Confederate soldiers had spotted Union horsemen on Cashtown Road, just northwest of the city of Gettysburg, Pennsylvania. By day's end, the rebel forces had pushed the Union army south of the city and pinned them into defensive positions on Culp's Hill and Cemetery Hill. By day three, at three in the afternoon, General Robert E. Lee ordered Confederate soldiers to attack the center of the Union line in what became the ill-fated "Pickett's Charge." When General George Pickett's men mounted the assault, they ran into a wall of withering artillery and musket fire from Union general Gordon Meade's troops. When the smoke cleared, an estimated fifty thousand bodies lay strewn on the battlefield.

As was customary during this period, particularly during the first two years of the Civil War, soldiers were frequently buried in the place they had been killed in battle, often in graves that had been haphazardly marked. But all this would soon change when Andrew G. Curtin, the Republican governor of Pennsylvania, toured the Gettysburg battlefield with David Wills, a prominent local attorney. Historian Ronald C. White Jr. describes what Curtin and Wills saw on July 10, 1863, as well as what this scene spurred them to do:

> They observed that graves were crudely marked, here by a piece of fencing, there by boards from ammunition or cracker boxes. Before returning to Harrisburg, Curtin asked Wills to be his agent, taking charge of plans to properly bury the dead even as farmers sought to resume their farming in these same fields. The diligent Wills became a prime mover in formulating plans for a national cemetery for a national army. He accumulated possession of seventeen acres for the new cemetery. The governors of all eighteen states in the Union were contacted. An interstate commission was formed. . . . The decision was made early on that such a national cemetery required a national dedication.[3]

The event planners, headed by Wills, wanted to secure Edward Everett as the keynote speaker. Everett was a man of great accomplishment and oratorical skill. He boasted an impressive resume: a former president of Harvard College, a former U.S. senator for the state of Massachusetts, and a former secretary of state. But when organizers contacted Everett a month before the originally planned October 23 event, Everett, ever the perfectionist, quickly replied that a month was hardly enough time for him to research and prepare his speech. November 19, said Everett, would be the preferred date to present a speech of this magnitude.[4] Thus the date was set.

Lincoln did not receive his official invitation to speak until just seventeen days before the event. Lincoln had not been invited to deliver a formal oration, but "as Chief Executive of the nation, [to] formally set apart these grounds to their sacred use by a few appropriate remarks." The president's invitation was likely preceded by backchannel communications through Lincoln's close friend and associate, Ward Hill Lamon, whom organizers had selected to serve as the grand marshal of the procession at Gettysburg, most likely because of his closeness to the president.[5] Popular myth holds that Lincoln dashed off the Gettysburg Address on the back of an envelope en route to the speech. This is entirely false. While many of Lincoln's early prepresidential speeches had been delivered impromptu, his presidential addresses were carefully crafted. And so it was with the Gettysburg Address. Almost from the moment he received the formal invitation, Lincoln devoted serious time and attention to the remarks he would deliver at the dedication of the new national cemetery. He even employed the counsel of White House landscape architect William Saunders to learn the topography of the location where he would soon speak. Using White House stationery, Lincoln began to write.[6]

At only 272 words in length, the Gettysburg Address draws its historic power from at least three central features of its design. The first and most structurally pervasive of these elements is Lincoln's use of life-cycle metaphors that build a temporal organizational pattern throughout the speech's introduction, body, and conclusion. These metaphors have the effect of taking the listener from the past to the present and into the future. Collectively, these metaphors conceptualize the nation as a living entity that must be nurtured, protected, and defended. In the *prooemium* (introduction) of the Gettysburg Address, for example,

Lincoln says that the nation had been "*conceived* in Liberty"; later, in the body of the speech he repeats the word *conceived* and then states that dedicating a portion of the battlefield is critical because the men who fought and died at Gettysburg had done so "that that nation might *live*"; and then in his epilogue (closure), the Republican president declares that these men had not died in vain, but had instead died so that the new nation could experience a "new *birth* of freedom" in order that that nation would not "*perish*" from the earth.

The second structural feature of Lincoln's speech—its use of biblical allusion and religious symbolism—builds off the first. By patterning his speech after the life cycle, not only had Lincoln used a chronological sequence from "conception" to "living" to "rebirth" but he had also embedded his deep Christian belief in the afterlife into the text. Like the Christian believer, Lincoln argued, the nation's sin of slavery could be washed clean so that the nation could experience salvation and thus experience a "new birth" (as in the modern locution "born-again Christian") so that the nation "shall not perish" (eternal life).

The structure of Lincoln's speech wasn't the only thing that was suffused with Christian belief. The words themselves radiated biblical tones and truths. Arguably the most famous six words of any American presidential speech, "Four score and seven years ago" was not only an attention-getting way of saying "eighty-seven years ago" but it also echoed the King James version of Psalm 90:10: "The days of our years are threescore years and ten; and if by reason of strength they be fourscore years, yet is their strength labor and sorrow." In reference to the spiritual quality of Lincoln's speech opener, rhetoric critic Edwin Black notes, "The first paragraph of the Gettysburg Address seems addressed to the ages. Lincoln does not imply a particular audience. He speaks the voice of omniscience."[7]

But beyond the religious-laden structure of his speech, Lincoln's lexical choices were sure to resonate with an audience steeped in Christianity. One of the most striking examples of this occurs in the president's use of a *scala*, a rhetorical device that uses words of ascending importance to create an upward moving staircaselike structure, as in Lincoln's memorable line "But, in a sense, we can not dedicate—

we can not consecrate—we can not hallow—this ground." To *dedicate* something means to set it apart for God's purposes. To *consecrate* it involves the process of sanctification or making it sacred, as in the preparation of the Eucharist elements in Communion. But to *hallow* something means to render it "holy." In this way, Lincoln's line creates a crescendo of spiritual significance for the president's Christian listeners.

In his prepared text, the president had not originally included the phrase "under God." Instead, rather unlike Lincoln, he added those words either just before the speech or during his delivery. What is clear is that Lincoln made certain that the three subsequent copies he prepared at later dates reflected his decision to include the phrase "that this nation, under God, shall have a new birth of freedom."[8]

Religious expressions made during funerals were hardly new. Neither was the model for eulogies. Indeed it was Pericles's Funeral Oration that had set the standard for funeral speeches to come. Pericles's funeral speech had praised not only the dead Athenian soldiers during the Peloponnesian War, but it had also praised the democratic ideals for which Athens stood. In elevating Athens, Pericles explained, citizens would elevate the men who died on its behalf: "I have dwelt upon the greatness of Athens because I want to show you that we are contending for a higher prize than those who enjoy none of these privileges, and to establish by manifest proof the merit of these men whom I am now commemorating. Their loftiest praise has been already spoken. For in magnifying the city I have magnified them, and men like them whose virtues made her glorious."

In speaking about the nation, Lincoln had been in keeping with the Athenian tradition set by Pericles. What differed, what made Lincoln's approach unique, was his application of Christian doctrine to a nonhuman entity, such as the nation. In this way, the Gettysburg Address is better understood as a speech focused on the transmogrification of a set of disparate, bloodied, sin-drenched states into a purified, unified nation. Thus, the salvation of which Lincoln spoke was directed at the *nation*, a term he uses five times throughout his address, not at the individuals he eulogized.

In addition, Lincoln's use of strategic ambiguity gives the speech its timeless quality. His lack of specificity, once considered, is quite striking and further confirms that Lincoln intended his speech to be a political reaffirmation of the morality of the Civil War just as much as a solemn dedication. Specific references to battles or individuals or even the actual location of which he speaks are nowhere to be found. "His tone was deliberately abstract," writes Pulitzer Prize–winning historian David Herbert Donald. "He made no specific reference to either the battle of Gettysburg or of the cemetery that he was dedicating, he did not mention the South or the Confederacy, and he did not speak of the Army of the Potomac or of its commanders. He was deliberately moving away from the particular occasion to make a general argument."[9]

Finally, blending both life-cycle metaphors with biblical allusions and symbols, Lincoln used antitheses to drive home the Civil War's stark moral stakes. With hundreds of thousands of deaths piling up over four years, the scourge of slavery had to be cast in the clearest of moral terms. For rhetoricians, the juxtaposition of oppositional forces is best accomplished through the use of antitheses—sentences that place antonyms in close proximity in order to create a striking contrast that grabs attention. This black-and-white vision of the moral universe leaves little room for gray. So, for example, Lincoln's antitheses involved opposites, such as *living* versus *dead*, *add* versus *detract*, *remember* versus *forget*, and *birth* versus *perish*. Each of these constructions further emphasizes the clarity of purpose and unequivocal nature of Lincoln's belief about the rightness of his cause.

On the day of the cemetery dedication, an estimated nine thousand people had formed a thick half-circle around the twelve-by-twenty-foot wooden platform from which Everett and President Lincoln would speak. Lincoln had spent the night before at David Wills's home. Following breakfast, the president and an entourage of governors, congressmen, military leaders, and cabinet officers had all made their entry into the venue on horseback. Lincoln's horse was chestnut in color and short in stature. So short, in fact, that observers recalled that the president's long, lanky legs seemed to drag on the ground as his horse clopped along.[10]

Although it was a solemn occasion, well-wishers crowded Lincoln, greeting him with handshakes. Lincoln wore his trademark black suit and black silk stovepipe hat with a mourning band in honor of his son Willie. At the speaker's platform, Lincoln was forced to wait for Everett to arrive. Everett, who suffered from bladder dysfunction, had arranged for a small tent to be placed near the platform in case he had to relieve himself; he knew how long he planned to talk, and there was no telling how long Lincoln might speak or how long it might take to wade through the sea of spectators who had gathered for the occasion.[11]

When Everett finally delivered his two-hour-and-eight-minute oration, he did so from memory. His speech manuscript, which lay unused on a nearby table, was over thirteen thousand words in length. The speech had been wrought and delivered in what ancient rhetoricians called "the grand style." Typified by its emphasis on ornate language, Everett's speech had been a study in detail and precision, further evidence of his trademark research and preparation. In fact, Everett had been so meticulous that he had spent three days before his speech surveying the battlefield terrain to check every detail and topographical reference to ensure the authenticity and accuracy of his descriptions. No less a powerful orator than John Quincy Adams, "Old Man Eloquent," as he was often called, once said that Everett's orations were "among the best ever delivered in this country and would stand the test of time."[12]

No sooner had Everett concluded his florid, baroque address than did Lincoln, with merely 272 words, whisk away a bygone era of old-style oratory and usher in the so-called plain style, a public speaking style Americans know well today. Lincoln's Gettysburg Address, one could say, was the genesis of the modern sound-bite culture. It wasn't that economy of language was new; rather, it was that it had long been ignored in favor of the more embellished style.[13] So terse was Lincoln's Gettysburg Address that when a photographer at the foot of the speaking platform had made the unfortunate decision to reset his equipment at the start of the president's speech, Lincoln had already concluded his remarks before the photographer could snap his first picture.

The brevity of the president's address stunned members of his audience. The hotels had been packed the night before; audience members had stood and waited for hours for the event to begin, even before Everett's two-hour address. Even the preacher's opening prayer had been longer than Lincoln's speech. And then, as audience members were settling in for another lengthy stem-winder like Everett's, in less than three minutes the towering president had said something about "government of the people, by the people, for the people," stopped speaking, and sat down. That was it. Nothing more. The audience had been so awestruck by the extreme brevity of Lincoln's speech that they had hesitated an unusually long time before applauding. Perhaps because of this, Lincoln had immediately felt his speech a failure. "Lamon," the president said aloud to his friend, "that speech won't *scour*! It is a flat failure, and the people are disappointed."[14]

But Everett's oratorical sensibilities told him otherwise. The day following their joint appearance, the magnanimous Everett wrote Lincoln a letter: "Permit me . . . to express my great admiration of the thoughts expressed by you, with such eloquent simplicity & appropriateness, at the consecration of the cemetery. I should be glad, if I could flatter myself, that I came as near to the central idea of the occasion, in two hours, as you did in two minutes."[15] In reply, an equally gracious Lincoln wrote, "Your kind note of today is received. In our respective parts yesterday, you could not have been excused to make a short address, nor I a long one. I am pleased to know that, in your judgment, the little I did say was not entirely a failure. Of course, I knew Mr. Everett would not fail, and yet, while the whole discourse was eminently satisfactory, and will be of great value, there were passages in it which transcended my expectations."[16]

Despite Lincoln's harsh self-critique, newspaper accounts of the Gettysburg Address varied widely. In his analysis of newspaper responses to the president's speech, Ronald F. Reid finds that, not surprisingly, Everett's speech received almost double the commentary as

Lincoln's. The historically partisan nature of newspapers was also reflected in the coverage: 40 percent of pro-administration "Republican" papers featured Lincoln's speech on the front page versus only 14 percent of the antiadministration newspapers.[17] Still, despite the smattering of positive and glowing reviews, the grandeur and gravity of Lincoln's Gettysburg Address would only grow henceforth.

As Edwin Black observes, the Gettysburg Address "is not just a vindication of the Civil War, or a poem to democracy, or a meditation on the legacies of the dead and the obligations of the living. It is also a map and a chronicle: it locates a burial ground in relation to all of space, and it fixes that moment of location in relation to all of time."[18] Lincoln's speech was just as much a political defense of his administration's war policies as it was a declaration of his commitment to democratic self-governance. But it was his use of life-cycle metaphors animated by both biblical allusion and antithetical sentence structures that made his address the magisterial marvel it became.

When Lincoln's special four-car presidential train brought him to Gettysburg the day before his speech, Lincoln stepped off the locomotive only to see hundreds of coffins on the train station platform. Just weeks before the cemetery dedication, the battlefield-turned-graveyard was still littered with fragments of human bone and hair belonging to the over fifty thousand men who fell there. But Lincoln felt right at home in such a place. Like the birth-death juxtapositions that filled his speech, Lincoln's melancholy life and deep spiritual faith had steeled him. They had allowed him to accept the inevitability of death as a necessary and essential part of rebirth and salvation, both of the human and the national souls.

Some things, Lincoln believed, were worth fighting and dying for.

Second Inaugural

MARCH 4, 1865

U.S. CAPITOL, WASHINGTON, D.C.

That was a sacred effort.

—Frederick Douglass, Republican and former slave,
commenting on Lincoln's second inaugural

Fellow Countrymen:

At this second appearing to take the oath of the presidential office, there is less occasion for an extended address than there was at the first. Then a statement, somewhat in detail, of a course to be pursued, seemed fitting and proper. Now, at the expiration of four years, during which public declarations have been constantly called forth on every point and phase of the great contest which still absorbs the attention, and engrosses the energies of the nation, little that is new could be presented. The progress of our arms, upon which all else chiefly depends, is as well known to the public as to myself; and it is, I trust, reasonably satisfactory and encouraging to all. With high hope for the future, no prediction in regard to it is ventured.

On the occasion corresponding to this four years ago, all thoughts were anxiously directed to an impending civil-war. All dreaded it—all sought to avert it. While the inaugural address was being delivered from this place, devoted altogether to saving the Union without war, insurgent agents were in the city seeking to destroy it without war—seeking to dissolve the Union, and divide effects, by negotiation. Both parties deprecated war; but one of them would make war rather than let the nation survive; and the other would accept war rather than let it perish. And the war came.

One eighth of the whole population were colored slaves, not distributed generally over the Union, but localized in the Southern part of it. These slaves constituted a peculiar and powerful interest. All knew that this interest was, somehow, the cause of the war. To strengthen, perpetuate, and extend this interest was the object for which the insurgents would rend the Union, even by war; while the government claimed no right to do more than to restrict the territorial enlargement of it. Neither party expected for the war, the magnitude, or the duration, which it has already attained. Neither anticipated that the cause of the conflict might cease with, or even before, the conflict itself should cease. Each looked for an easier triumph, and a result less fundamental and astounding. Both read the same Bible, and pray to the same God; and each invokes His aid against the other.

It may seem strange that any men should dare to ask a just God's assistance in wringing their bread from the sweat of other men's faces; but let us judge not that we be not judged. The prayers of both could not be answered; that of neither has been answered fully. The Almighty has His own purposes. "Woe unto the world because of offences! For it must needs be that offences come; but woe to that man by whom the offence cometh!"

If we shall suppose that American Slavery is one of those offences which, in the providence of God, must needs come, but which, having continued through His appointed time, He now wills to remove, and that He gives to both North and South, this terrible war, as the woe due to those by whom the offence came, shall we discern therein any departure from those divine *attributes which the believers in a Living God always ascribe to Him? Fondly do we hope—fervently do we pray—that this mighty scourge of war may speedily pass away. Yet, if God wills that it continue, until all the wealth piled by the bond-man's two hundred and fifty years of unrequited toil shall be sunk, and until every drop of blood drawn with the lash, shall be paid by another drawn with the sword, as was said three thousand years ago, so still it must be said "the judgments of the Lord, are true and righteous altogether."*

With malice toward none; with charity for all; with firmness in the right, as God gives us to see the right, let us strive on to finish the work we are in; to bind up the nation's wounds; to care for him who shall have borne the battle, and for his widow, and his orphan to do all which may achieve and cherish a just, and a lasting peace, among ourselves, and with all nations.

On the morning of March 4, 1865, Frederick Douglass, a lifelong Republican and former slave turned Abolitionist leader, trudged his way through the wet Washington streets alongside the estimated fifty thousand citizens who had assembled at the Capitol to watch the second inauguration of Abraham Lincoln. As the era's leading black orator, Douglass had grown accustomed to standing behind the lectern, often advancing the cause of the Republican Party. But on this day he was a spectator. He had come to listen.

Douglass's commitment to the Republican Party was no secret: "I am a Republican, a black, dyed in the wool Republican, and I never intend to belong to any other party than the party of freedom and progress," he declared. Indeed, so sweeping was black support for the Grand Old Party (GOP) that of the over fifteen hundred black office-holders of the Reconstruction period, only fifteen were Democrats.[19] The reason? Like Douglass, black Americans had seen their Republican Party fight Democrats and the Ku Klux Klan, an organization that University of North Carolina emeritus professor of history William Trelease notes was "the terrorist arm of the Democratic

Party." Moreover, African Americans of the period knew their history. They had watched Republicans fight for and pass sweeping historic civil rights victories, including the Thirteenth, Fourteenth, and Fifteenth Amendments; the Civil Rights Act of 1865; the First Reconstruction Act of 1867; the Ku Klux Klan Act of 1871; and the Civil Rights Act of 1875.[20]

But on this day, Douglass had braved the unrelenting rains to see his fellow Republican and friend Abraham Lincoln deliver what would become the most famous presidential inaugural address in U.S. history. Following an embarrassing, drunken ramble of an oration by Andrew Johnson, his Democratic vice president, Lincoln leaned over to the parade marshal and whispered, "Do not let Johnson speak outside." After being introduced, Lincoln stood up, put on his steel-rimmed eyeglasses, and walked up to the white iron table that served as a lectern. Looking out over the ocean of faces that had assembled to see him speak, the president's eyes found Douglass's face in the crowd. That Douglass and the other black citizens had been permitted to participate in the ceremonies was somewhat unusual; blacks had been barred from attending previous inaugural festivities. But Douglass figured "it was not too great an assumption for a colored man to offer his congratulations to the President with those of other citizens."[21] So he went.

Also in the crowd had been myriad soldiers, fresh from Civil War battlefields and hospitals. The fact that many were amputees made them painfully easy to spot. Indeed, 75 percent of all Civil War surgeries were amputations. Citizens assembled for Lincoln's second inaugural had been shocked to see scores of soldiers missing arms and legs in the audience.[22] The words the president would soon speak, however, had been constructed to address both the literal and symbolic wounds of the nation. And like the Gettysburg Address, Lincoln's speech would depend heavily on his infusion of Christianity and biblical references as he sought to unite both North and South, even as Confederates were in the last throes of rebellion.

.   .   .

At the exact moment that President Lincoln began delivering his second inaugural, the cloud-covered skies parted and allowed a burst of sunshine to beam through. Later that day Chief Justice Salmon P. Chase, who would administer the oath of office to Lincoln, wrote to Mary Todd Lincoln, Lincoln's wife, that "the beautiful sunshine" breaking through the clouds had been "an auspicious omen of the dispersion of the clouds of war and the restoration of the clear sunlight of prosperous peace under the wise & just administration of him who took" the oath of office. Likewise, Lincoln later told a friend that he was "just superstitious enough to consider it a happy omen."[23] Lincoln began:

> *At this second appearing to take the oath of the presidential office, there is less occasion for an extended address than there was at the first. Then a statement, somewhat in detail, of a course to be pursued, seemed fitting and proper. Now, at the expiration of four years, during which public declarations have been constantly called forth on every point and phase of the great contest which still absorbs the attention, and engrosses the energies of the nation, little that is new could be presented. The progress of our arms, upon which all else chiefly depends, is as well known to the public as to myself; and it is, I trust, reasonably satisfactory and encouraging to all. With high hope for the future, no prediction in regard to it is ventured.*

These beginning words of Lincoln's 703-word speech, the second-shortest inaugural address in U.S. history, did not portend a great oration. As rhetoric scholar Michael Leff observed, "the opening paragraph contains no striking ideas or stylistic flourishes, in fact, it has a somewhat awkward appearance."[24] Yet the lackluster, deflated, impersonal opening had the effect of directing focus away from Lincoln and toward uniting the nation.

> *On the occasion corresponding to this four years ago, all thoughts were anxiously directed to an impending civil-war. All dreaded*

*it—all sought to avert it. While the inaugural address was being
delivered from this place, devoted altogether to saving the Union
without war, insurgent agents were in the city seeking to destroy
it without war—seeking to dissolve the Union, and divide
effects, by negotiation. Both parties deprecated war; but one of
them would make war rather than let the nation survive; and
the other would accept war rather than let it perish. And the war
came.*

The magnanimity of such a passage should be clear. With limbless
Union soldiers hobbling about the Capitol, Lincoln's refusal to
directly and unequivocally assign blame to Confederate states for
the mass deaths the Union suffered all but ran the risk of offending
Northern segments of his audience. But Lincoln was intent on striking an inclusive tone. Therefore, he used ambiguity as a form of abso-
lution, as a way of "getting on with it." Nowhere does the president
specify *which* party "made war" and which one "accepted it." All
along, the president had desired to thrust the nation beyond the
bloody conflict over slavery to a place of healing and reconciliation.
So much so, in fact, that Lincoln made a point of visiting both Union
and Confederate soldiers in the hospitals throughout Washington.

Still, Union supporters had a right to feel jilted; the war had
lasted far longer than any had expected, largely because of the rebels'
refusal to stop fighting, thus resulting in far greater total casualties
for the North than the South. Lincoln's conciliatory tone led
Republican leaders such as Pennsylvania congressman Thaddeus
Stevens to forcefully lobby the president to not make too hasty and
painless a peace with the South. Stevens wanted Lincoln to rub
Southerners' faces in the sin of slavery. He wanted to force them to
"eat the fruit of foul rebellion." When the congressman said this,
Lincoln looked at him for a moment in silence before replying,
"Stevens, this is a pretty big hog we are trying to catch, and to hold
when we do catch him."[25]

Eschewing what must have been an enormous political temptation
to scapegoat the causes, the war, and the immorality of slavery solely

on the South, Lincoln instead chose to share responsibility for the conflict in an effort to begin suturing the wounds of a riven nation. Even in that most powerful and famous last line of the passage—"And the war came"—Lincoln speaks as if the war were somehow inevitable, like an unavoidable natural disaster. Indeed, as Lincoln soon makes clear, that is precisely what the president suggests the Civil War may very well have been: a God-ordained punishment for the national sin of slavery.

> One eighth of the whole population were colored slaves, not distributed generally over the Union, but localized in the Southern part of it. These slaves constituted a peculiar and powerful interest. All knew that this interest was, somehow, the cause of the war. To strengthen, perpetuate, and extend this interest was the object for which the insurgents would rend the Union, even by war; while the government claimed no right to do more than to restrict the territorial enlargement of it. Neither party expected for the war, the magnitude, or the duration, which it has already attained. Neither anticipated that the cause of the conflict might cease with, or even before, the conflict itself should cease. Each looked for an easier triumph, and a result less fundamental and astounding. Both read the same Bible, and pray to the same God; and each invokes His aid against the other.
>
> It may seem strange that any men should dare to ask a just God's assistance in wringing their bread from the sweat of other men's faces; but let us judge not that we be not judged. The prayers of both could not be answered; that of neither has been answered fully. The Almighty has His own purposes. "Woe unto the world because of offences! For it must needs be that offences come; but woe to that man by whom the offence cometh!"

This passage sees the introduction of a barrage of biblical references woven together with the theological conundrums Lincoln saw running through the conflict. In total, the second inaugural contains fourteen references to God (or some variation, as in "Almighty" or "His") and four direct quotes from the Bible. This passage, perhaps more than any other, fuses Lincoln's forgiving rhetoric of reconciliation with biblical insights and mysteries. Moreover, the use of words such as *both* as well as *and* further collapsed the divide between both sides, because they suggested a sameness, a oneness that mirrored the idea that all citizens are children of God who "read the same Bible, and pray to the same God."

Lincoln's first use of scripture came from Genesis 3:19; it was the closest he came to scolding the South for using prayer as a mechanism to maintain the institution of slavery. In the King James Version, Genesis 3:19 reads: "In the sweat of thy face shalt thou eat bread, till thou return unto the ground; for out of it wast thou taken: for dust thou art, and unto dust shalt thou return." By prefacing his biblical reference with "it may seem strange that any men should dare," Lincoln had delivered a rhetorical clenched fist wrapped in a velvet glove by suggesting that Confederate conceptions of Christianity as being compatible with slavery was "strange." Some scholars, such as Martha Solomon, suggest that Lincoln's rhetorical move represents a form of "moral hegemony" against the South.[26] But when considered alongside the president's next biblical reference, such a view seems overstated.

In the same sentence, the president pulls back the reins of indignation against Southern invocations of religion to preserve slavery. Citing Matthew 7:1, Lincoln said, "But let us judge not that we be not judged." Having planted the seed of Southern theological bastardization, Lincoln tempers the earlier half of the sentence by suggesting that it is not the place of humans to sit in judgment over God's designs. But he doesn't stop there. The president then shifts his focus to scold both sides for believing that God fully and completely favored one side over the other. Lincoln's is not a message of moral relativism, however. Far from it. He makes it clear that he believes God has a Divine purpose, plan, and will ("The Almighty has His own purposes"). But Lincoln also believed that man does not possess the intellectual capacity or spiritual knowledge required to decipher God's desires.

Finally, while warning against the temptation of hubris or moral superiority, Lincoln reminded the nation that sin is not without consequence. Underscoring God's abhorrence of sin, the president referenced Matthew 18:7: "Woe unto the world because of offences! For it must needs be that offences come; but woe to that man by whom the offence cometh!" This biblical reference concludes this passage and acts as a bridge into the next:

> If we shall suppose that American Slavery is one of those offences which, in the providence of God, must needs come, but which, having continued through His appointed time, He now wills to remove, and that He gives to both North and South, this terrible war, as the woe due to those by whom the offence came, shall we discern therein any departure from those divine attributes which the believers in a Living God always ascribe to Him? Fondly do we hope—fervently do we pray—that this mighty scourge of war may speedily pass away. Yet, if God wills that it continue, until all the wealth piled by the bond-man's two hundred and fifty years of unrequited toil shall be sunk, and until every drop of blood drawn with the lash, shall be paid by another drawn with the sword, as was said three thousand years ago, so still it must be said "the judgments of the Lord, are true and righteous altogether."

This second to last passage is remarkable on several levels. First, by saying "*American* Slavery" [emphasis mine], Lincoln underscores his inclusive theme. As Ronald C. White Jr. notes, Lincoln "could have said 'slavery' or 'Southern slavery,' or simply located slaves as residing in the South. Instead he uses the inclusive *American Slavery*."[27] In this way, Lincoln refuses to let the North off the moral hook; he seems to be saying that sins of omission (North) are no less repugnant in the eyes of God than sins of commission (South).

Second, having already in the first paragraph buffered against grand declarations or predictions that the war is in its final gasps—"With

high hope for the future, no prediction in regard to it is ventured"—
Lincoln inoculates his military strategy against future criticism should
the war languish on. By casting the "terrible war" and "mighty
scourge of war" as forms of God's punishment and retributive justice
for slavery, Lincoln attempts to silence both North and South from
further critique of his administration. After all, Lincoln's argument
goes, every drop of blood spilled by the slave owner's whip is even
now being repaid by the blood spilled on the battlefield. Similar to the
theme he developed at Gettysburg, Lincoln was saying that while the
war may have begun as a way to preserve the Union, God may also
have used the war to end and cleanse the nation of the unrighteous-
ness of slavery. Moreover, he suggests, it is not the right of humans to
question the purposes of God. Thus, "in destroying slavery, the war to
save the Union had been worth the heavy cost. God in His wisdom
had made it so."[28]

> *With malice toward none; with charity for all; with firmness in
> the right, as God gives us to see the right, let us strive on to fin-
> ish the work we are in; to bind up the nation's wounds; to care
> for him who shall have borne the battle, and for his widow, and
> his orphan to do all which may achieve and cherish a just, and
> a lasting peace, among ourselves, and with all nations.*

In this, the most famous and quoted of passages from the second
inaugural, Lincoln's lead antithesis juxtaposes the words *none* and *all*
to further emphasize the inclusive, unifying theme developed
throughout the speech. By making the nation a metaphorical patient
in need of bandaging, as well as stressing the need to "care for him
who shall have borne the battle, and for his widow, and his orphan,"
Lincoln's line must have been especially moving for his audience, as
many in the crowd were literally shoulder to shoulder with amputee
veterans. Concern for the widows and orphans of soldiers—both
Union and Confederate—was a message that transcended the conflict. What's more, he completes the final stop on his temporal time
line that went from past to present to future with the words "let us

strive on to finish." He also balances moral clarity ("with firmness in the right") with Christian humility ("as God gives us to see the right"). As historian Doris Kearns Goodwin notes, "More than any of his other speeches, the Second Inaugural fused spiritual faith with politics."[29]

Newspaper coverage, while generally favorable, predictably broke mostly along partisan lines, just as it had with Lincoln's address at Gettysburg. But it had been the praise of one member of Lincoln's audience that had mattered most to him: his fellow Republican and friend, Frederick Douglass. At a White House reception following the president's speech, Lincoln stood shaking the hands of a long line of well-wishers who had come to congratulate him. At one point in the party, someone notified Lincoln that Douglass was at the front door, but that police had stopped the former slave from entering because he was black. Douglass describes in moving detail what happened next:

> I told the officers I was quite sure there must be some mistake, for no such order could have emanated from President Lincoln; and if he knew I was at the door he would desire my admission. They then . . . assumed an air of politeness, and offered to conduct me in. We followed their lead, and soon found ourselves walking some planks out of a window, which had been arranged as a temporary passage for the exit of visitors. . . . I said to the officers: "You have deceived me. I shall not go out of this building till I see President Lincoln." At this moment a gentleman who was passing in, recognized me, and I said to him: "Be so kind as to say to Mr. Lincoln that Frederick Douglass is detained by officers at the door."
>
> It was not long before Mrs. Dorsey and I walked into the spacious East Room, amid a scene of elegance such as in this country I had never witnessed before. Like a mountain pine high above all others, Mr. Lincoln stood,

in his grand simplicity, and homelike beauty, recognizing me, even before I reached him, he exclaimed, so that all around could hear him, "Here comes my friend Douglass!" Taking me by the hand, he said, "I am glad to see you. I saw you in the crowd today, listening to my inaugural address; how did you like it?" I said, "Mr. Lincoln, I must not detain you with my poor opinion, when there are thousands waiting to shake hands with you." "No, no," he said, "you must stop a little, Douglass; there is no man in the country whose opinion I value more than yours. I want to know what you think of it." I replied, "Mr. Lincoln, that was a sacred effort." "I am glad you liked it!" he said, and I passed on, feeling that any man, however distinguished, might well regard himself honored by such expressions, from such a man.[30]

In a letter written to Thurlow Weed the day after his speech, Lincoln confessed that he believed his second inaugural was possibly the best speech of his career. Lincoln said that while many might not warm to it immediately, his speech had placed himself and the Republican Party on the right side of history: "I expect the latter [speech] to wear as well as—perhaps better than—anything I have produced; but I believe it is not immediately popular. Men are not flattered by being shown that there has been a difference of purpose between the Almighty and them. To deny it, however, in this case, is to deny that there is a God governing the world."[31]

— 2 —

Theodore Roosevelt

The Rough-Riding Rhetorician

The Strenuous Life

APRIL 10, 1899

THE HAMILTON CLUB, CHICAGO, ILLINOIS

———————

It is hard to fail, but it is worse never to have tried to succeed.
In this life we get nothing save by effort.

—Theodore Roosevelt

As with just about everything else in Theodore Roosevelt's life, learning to deliver public speeches had been an act of individual will and self-determination. The Rough Rider turned president didn't so much deliver an oration as muscle his words around before shoving them out of his mouth. Indeed, watching the five-foot eight-inch two-hundred-plus-pound president deliver an oration was a sight to behold. The barrel-chested Roosevelt wore wire-rimmed eyeglasses, jabbed his finger at the audience when emphasizing a point, and often flashed that broad smile with teeth so prominent they resembled large white tiles. Ironically, his vocal quality didn't match his robust physical appearance. Historian Candice Millard wrote that Roosevelt's voice "sounded as if he had just taken a sip of helium."[1]

Having endured an agonizing childhood wracked by illness, Roosevelt was lucky his audience could hear him at all. "I was a sickly, delicate boy, suffered much from asthma," Roosevelt remembered in his autobiography, "and frequently had to be taken away on trips to find a place where I could breathe."[2] So bad and all-encompassing was his condition that he could not attend public schools as a child. Worse, his extreme near sightedness had gone undiagnosed until his teen years. "I could not see and yet was wholly ignorant that I was not seeing," he wrote.[3]

He recalled that in his youth he had endured teasing and bullying that had "proceeded to make life miserable." When Roosevelt had dared to fight back on one occasion, the bully handled him easily. But instead of being discouraged by the experience, Roosevelt was inspired:

> The experience taught me what probably no amount of good advice could have taught me. I made up my mind that I must try to learn so that I would not again be put in such a helpless position; and having become quickly and bitterly conscious that I did not have the natural prowess to hold my own, I decided that I would try to supply its place by training. . . . I started to learn to box. I was a painfully slow and awkward pupil, and certainly worked two or three years before I made any perceptible improvement whatever.[4]

Roosevelt did not become a great athlete, but as a wrestler and boxer at Harvard he proved to himself and others that he could overcome his physical maladies and stand on his own. For Roosevelt, that had been the point all along: "I felt a great admiration for men who were fearless and who could hold their own in the world, and I had a great desire to be like them."[5]

When confronted with obstacles and challenges—personal or national—Roosevelt followed a predictable pattern: run *toward* them, not away from them. His belief in the power of the individual to alter his own surroundings and change his own destiny was boundless. Roosevelt believed that a strong work ethic and gritty, vigorous determination could overcome most of life's obstacles. The celebration of individualism remains a key feature of Republican Party phi-

losophy and rhetoric today. As a Republican message of individualism, military strength, and self-reliance, Roosevelt's words contained
added velocity because, despite being born to a family of privilege,
Roosevelt had lived the principles he espoused. Roosevelt's life and
words would later inspire other maverick Republican spokesmen of
individualism, such as Barry Goldwater and John McCain. Yet,
Roosevelt's speech on April 10, 1899, remains one of the clearest
Republican declarations of how work, individualism, and tradition
should guide American citizens and the national government that
serves them.

By the time Roosevelt delivered the Strenuous Life to the Hamilton Club, a group, according to the *Federal Observer*, whose members
represented the "hard core of Republican leadership in the 'capital of
the prairies,'"[6] he had already accomplished more than most people
accomplish in a lifetime: he had graduated Phi Beta Kappa from Harvard before going to Columbia Law School; at twenty-three he had
been elected to the New York state assembly; by twenty-six he was
appointed chairman of the state delegation to the Republican
National Convention in 1884; he served as a civil service commissioner under President Benjamin Harrison before becoming the
New York City police commissioner; as the leader of the Rough
Riders, he led a famous charge up San Juan Hill during the Spanish-
American War; he served as the assistant secretary of the navy; and at
forty-one he was elected the governor of New York. Soon, he would
become the youngest president in U.S. history. But on April 10, 1899,
the ambitious New York governor was busy preaching his vision of
masculine individualism, military readiness, and traditional virtue to
his fellow Republicans using the muscular prose that became his
trademark:

> *I wish to preach, not the doctrine of ignoble ease, but the doc-
> trine of the strenuous life, the life of toil and effort, of labor and
> strife; to preach that highest form of success which comes, not to
> the man who desires mere easy peace, but to the man who does*

not shrink from danger, from hardship, or from bitter toil, and who out of these wins the splendid ultimate triumph. A life of slothful ease, a life of that peace which springs merely from lack either of desire or of power to strive after great things, is as little worthy of a nation as of an individual. I ask only that what every self-respecting American demands from himself and from his sons shall be demanded of the American nation as a whole.

It was an odd way to begin a speech. While "preaching" may possess a negative connotation for modern ears, the same could not be said for those in Roosevelt's time. Indeed, Roosevelt famously called the American presidency the "bully pulpit." While Roosevelt's critics often charged that his public statements were overly bellicose, in fact, Roosevelt often used the word *bully* to mean "excellent," a fact often lost on and misinterpreted by individuals today. But by announcing in advance that he intended to exalt a life of "toil," "labor," and "hardship," Roosevelt's lugubrious opener had the effect of arresting the listener's attention, of making the audience lean forward in their seats. With the turn of the century just seven months away, and with his eyes fixed on the White House, Roosevelt was determined to offer his vision of what the United States could become if it embraced "the strenuous life."

The rhetorical challenge for Republicans then and now remains how to promote individualism and self-control while, at the same time, sounding themes of national, collective unity. Put another way, Republicans struggle to promote individualism while still tipping their rhetorical hats toward collectivist appeals of togetherness and a sense of community. Throughout his public life and prolific writings, Roosevelt overcame this challenge by stressing fair play and equal treatment, regardless of one's class or background. But more than that, in one form or another, Roosevelt's mantra was always "act, instead of criticize."[7] He believed that individual actions by individual citizens would yield the collective betterment of the nation. Hence, his rhetorical fusion of individualism and collective identity.

If you are rich and are worth your salt, you will teach your sons that though they may have leisure, it is not to be spent in idleness; for wisely used leisure merely means that those who possess it, being free from the necessity of working for their livelihood, are all the more bound to carry on some kind of non-remunerative work in science, in letters, in art, in exploration, in historical research—work of the type we most need in this country, the successful carrying out of which reflects most honor upon the nation. We do not admire the man of timid peace. We admire the man who embodies victorious effort; the man who never wrongs his neighbor, who is prompt to help a friend, but who has those virile qualities necessary to win in the stern strife of actual life. It is hard to fail, but it is worse never to have tried to succeed. In this life we get nothing save by effort. Freedom from effort in the present merely means that there has been stored up effort in the past. A man can be freed from the necessity of work only by the fact that he or his fathers before him have worked to good purpose.

This passage is strikingly autobiographical. Roosevelt possessed enormous reverence and affection for his father. As he stated in his autobiography, "My father, Theodore Roosevelt, was the best man I ever knew."[8] Yet on one issue Roosevelt differed from his father, and it is this instance that explains Roosevelt's thirst for the manly virtues and hunger to experience the rush of war and the thrill of battle. During the Civil War, the senior Roosevelt had paid another man to take his place on the battlefield to fight the Union cause, which he fervently supported. Hardly an act of cowardice, the practice was quite common among wealthy men. In the case of Roosevelt's father, his decision to hire a proxy soldier had also been an act of respect toward his wife and Roosevelt's mother, Martha Roosevelt, who was a Southern belle with two brothers fighting in the Confederate army. Yet despite his limitless respect and admiration for his father— "I am as much inferior to Father morally and mentally as physically"

Roosevelt had written in his diary—he could never accept his father's decision to, as he saw it, buy his way out of fighting.[9]

In his Pulitzer prize–winning biography of Theodore Roosevelt, historian Edmund Morris observes that Roosevelt made no mention of his father's role in the Civil War. As was his way, Roosevelt often ignored that which he found painful. Morris notes that, "[M]any biographers, including his own sister, have suggested that guilt over that substitute soldier explains the future Rough Rider's almost hysterical desire to wage war."[10] Interestingly, however, when an assassin's bullet took the life of President William McKinley, and thus elevated Roosevelt from vice president to president, not only did Roosevelt not ignite a major war during his eight years in office, but in September 1905 he mediated the end to the Russo-Japanese War, an effort for which he was later awarded the Nobel Peace Prize. Roosevelt's admonition to "speak softly and carry a big stick" had been an early version of Ronald Reagan's message that America must achieve "peace through strength." Yet at this stage of his address, Roosevelt was merely previewing the three themes of his speech: the moral virtue of individual work and striving, the folly of isolationism and need for martial dominance, and an exultation of tradition.

> *A healthy state can exist only when the men and women who make it up lead clean, vigorous, healthy lives. . . . The man must be glad to do a man's work, to dare and endure and to labor; to keep himself, and to keep those dependent upon him. The woman must be the housewife, the helpmeet of the homemaker, the wise and fearless mother of many healthy children. . . . When men fear work or fear righteous war, when women fear motherhood, they tremble on the brink of doom; and well it is that they should vanish from the earth, where they are fit subjects for the scorn of all men and women who are themselves strong and brave and high-minded.*
>
> *As it is with the individual, so it is with the nation.*

In words that make modern liberal feminists cringe, Roosevelt advocated a traditionalist view of gender roles in marriage. Such a view was certainly in keeping with the attitudes—both Republican and Democrat—of the time. But in his clarion call to fearless and courageous living, it is important to note that Roosevelt did not relegate "fearlessness" to the realm of men. Most important of all, Roosevelt advanced the argument that the nation's character is nothing more than the collective character of its individual citizens.

His strong emphasis on male responsibility extended beyond the battlefield. Roosevelt held to account those congressmen and other men who were patrons of the burlesque theaters and gambling rooms just blocks away from the White House. As for his own personal behavior, University of Texas professor Marvin Olasky notes that "Roosevelt himself did no prowling, even though it was the custom for many affluent men to have a mistress. He was authentically a family man in his forties with a loving wife and fun-loving children."[11]

If in 1861 the men who loved the Union had believed that peace was the end of all things, and war and strife the worst of all things, and had acted up to their belief, we would have saved hundreds of thousands of lives, we would have saved hundreds of millions of dollars. . . . We would have prevented the heartbreak of many women, the dissolution of many homes, and we would have spared the country those months of gloom and shame when it seemed as if our armies marched only to defeat. We could have avoided all this suffering simply by shrinking from strife. And if we had thus avoided it, we would have shown that we were weaklings, and that we were unfit to stand among the great nations of the earth. Thank God for the iron in the blood of our fathers, the men who upheld the wisdom of Lincoln, and bore sword or rifle in the armies of Grant! Let us, the children of the men who proved themselves equal to the mighty days, let us, the children of the men who carried the great Civil

War to a triumphant conclusion, praise the God of our fathers that the ignoble counsels of peace were rejected; that the suffering and loss, the blackness of sorrow and despair, were unflinchingly faced, and the years of strife endured; for in the end the slave was freed, the Union restored, and the mighty American republic placed once more as a helmeted queen among nations.

Speaking in Chicago, Illinois, the Land of Lincoln, Roosevelt's unbridled praise of the Union cause was a safe bet, as all in the room were northern Republicans. In this passage, governor Roosevelt forcefully argued that the use of war for liberation is not only permissible but also moral and just. What's more, he contended that inaction would have been "weak" and ignoble. Indeed, throughout his political life, Roosevelt had extended his bold leadership style to the cause of African American equality. And, as with so many of his other bold stands, Roosevelt had caused a stir. One of his first controversial moves as president occurred on October 16, 1901, when he invited Booker T. Washington to join him for dinner in the White House. Some southern white supremacists were so angered by the move that they responded with violent attacks against blacks.[12] But Roosevelt was a man of firm conviction. And it was Roosevelt's equating of individual virtue to national virtue—even that which requires war and mass death—that gave his message moral resonance with his immediate Republican audience, an audience that was, one must recall, only thirty-five years removed from the Civil War.

As the nations grow to have ever wider and wider interests, and are brought into closer and closer contact, if we are to hold our own in the struggle for naval and commercial supremacy, we must build up our power without our own borders. . . . Our army has never been built up as it should be built up. . . . If we are such weaklings as the proposition implies, then we are unworthy of freedom in any event. To no body of men in the United States is the country so much indebted as to the splen-

did officers and enlisted men of the regular army and navy. There is no body from which the country has less to fear, and none of which it should be prouder, none which it should be more anxious to upbuild.

Our army needs complete reorganization—not merely enlarging—and the reorganization can only come as the result of legislation. . . . Never again should we see, as we saw in the Spanish war, major-generals in command of divisions who had never before commanded three companies together in the field. Yet, incredible to relate, Congress has shown a queer inability to learn some of the lessons of the war. There were large bodies of men in both branches who opposed the declaration of war, who opposed the ratification of peace, who opposed the upbuilding of the army, and who even opposed the purchase of armor at a reasonable price for the battle-ships and cruisers, thereby putting an absolute stop to the building of any new fighting-ships for the navy. If, during the years to come, any disaster should befall our arms, afloat or ashore, and thereby any shame come to the United States, remember that the blame will lie upon the men whose names appear upon the roll-calls of Congress on the wrong side of these great questions. On them will lie the burden of any loss of our soldiers and sailors, of any dishonor to the flag; and upon you and the people of this country will lie the blame if you do not repudiate, in no unmistakable way, what these men have done. The blame will . . . [rest] upon the public men who have so lamentably failed in forethought as to refuse to remedy these evils long in advance, and upon the nation that stands behind those public men.

Not unlike the fierce budgetary battles that took place over the largest peacetime military buildup in U.S. history by President Reagan and Secretary of Defense Caspar Weinberger, so, too, had presidential hopeful Theodore Roosevelt presaged his intent to rejuvenate

U.S. military forces. The most visible of these efforts culminated in his "Great White Fleet," a fleet of sixteen U.S. battleships that departed from Hampton Roads in December 1907 for a forty-six-thousand-mile expedition. Indeed, the currency of Roosevelt's words to modern debates over military preparedness, weapons systems, and troop strength is striking. Politically, Roosevelt was positioning himself as *the* presidential candidate with the most credibility on military matters. But more than that, Roosevelt, the colonel and former assistant secretary of the navy, was warning that if some national calamity were to befall the United States, blood would be on the hands of those leaders who failed to put the United States on a path toward strength and security.

> *A man's first duty is to his own home, but he is not thereby excused from doing his duty to the State; for if he fails in this second duty it is under the penalty of ceasing to be a freeman. In the same way, while a nation's first duty is within its own borders, it is not thereby absolved from facing its duties in the world as a whole; and if it refuses to do so, it merely forfeits its right to struggle for a place among the peoples that shape the destiny of mankind.*

America's geographic location and rich natural resources have always invited isolationist temptation. But maintaining a strong military and well-funded defenses has historically meant rhetorically buffering against isolationist flirtation. To be sure, for a period many in the Republican Party, weary of two world wars, succumbed to the lure of isolationism. But from Lincoln to Roosevelt to Dwight D. Eisenhower to Reagan, Republicans have historically supported a strong national defense and eschewed a strictly isolationist foreign policy.

> *I preach to you, then, my countrymen, that our country calls not for the life of ease but for the life of strenuous endeavor. The twentieth century looms before us big with the fate of many*

nations. If we stand idly by, if we seek merely swollen, slothful ease and ignoble peace, if we shrink from the hard contests where men must win at hazard of their lives and at the risk of all they hold dear, then the bolder and stronger peoples will pass us by, and will win for themselves the domination of the world. Let us therefore boldly face the life of strife, resolute to do our duty well and manfully; resolute to uphold righteousness by deed and by word; resolute to be both honest and brave, to serve high ideals, yet to use practical methods. Above all, let us shrink from no strife, moral or physical, within or without the nation, provided we are certain that the strife is justified, for it is only through strife, through hard and dangerous endeavor, that we shall ultimately win the goal of true national greatness.

Roosevelt concluded the Strenuous Life with a final passage that encapsulated the great tension so often at work in Republican rhetoric: *national* virtue can only ever be achieved through *individual* virtue; the heavy lifting of history requires a watchful captain willing to voyage against the tides of collective ease. The subtext of Roosevelt's speech was that he was that captain. For many of the influential Republicans in the room, however, the young New York governor's rhetoric had struck them as being too bold, too brashly youthful and vigorous. So the decision was made to nominate him as vice president and thereby subsume him under the shadow of the more reserved and moderate William McKinley. It was a move many politically ambitious New York Republicans applauded. But the decision proved fateful. Following McKinley's assassination, the Rough Rider blazed into the Oval Office, where he preached the strenuous life from his presidential bully pulpit.

The Man with the Muck-Rake

APRIL 15, 1906

WASHINGTON, D.C.

_____

The foundation-stone of national life is, and ever must be,
the high individual character of the average citizen.

—Theodore Roosevelt

A little over a quarter of a century after Theodore Roosevelt's death, rhetoric critics like William A. Behl had already rendered their verdict: "The name of Theodore Roosevelt will not be remembered as that of a great orator; he was not a great orator."[13] The judgment was not without merit. Even early in his oratorical career, Roosevelt had struggled with public speaking. During Roosevelt's college years, for example, historian H. W. Brands records that Roosevelt had displayed "difficulty in enunciating clearly or even in running off his words smoothly." One audience member recalled that "[a]t times he could hardly get [the words] out at all, and then he would rush on for a few sentences, as skaters redouble their pace over thin ice." And journalist George Spinney said that "I always think of a man biting tenpenny nails when I think of Roosevelt making a speech."[14]

Roosevelt was not unaware of his rhetorical limitations. His high-pitched voice, short stature, and battle with asthma didn't help. What's more, he later lamented that during his time at Harvard College he had not studied elocution or participated in formal debate. This lack of preparation meant that he had been forced to teach himself the art of persuasion. While in the New York Assembly, Roosevelt said, "Like all young men, I had considerable difficulty in teaching myself to speak." He noted that one piece of advice given to him by a "hard-headed old countryman" had served him well: "Don't speak until you are sure you have something to say; then say it, and then sit down."[15]

More than even the mechanics of oral performance and delivery, what troubled Roosevelt most about public speaking had been the sophistic, "slippery" moral quality he detected in some speakers, especially lawyers, who could argue both sides of a case without compunction:

> I never studied elocution or practiced debating. This was a loss to me in one way. In another way it was not. Personally I have not the slightest sympathy with debating contests in which each side is arbitrarily assigned a given proposition and told to maintain it without the least reference to whether those maintaining it believe in it or not. I know that under our system this is necessary for lawyers, but I emphatically disbelieve in it as regards general discussion of political, social, and industrial matters. What we need is to turn out of our colleges young men with ardent convictions on the side of the right; not young men who can make a good argument for either right or wrong as their interest bids them.[16]

Roosevelt's sentiments regarding a morally grounded collegiate education mirrored the later reflections of William F. Buckley Jr., who lamented the erosion of ethics in higher education. Yet, Roosevelt's views also reflected an unyielding belief that the power of a speech was contingent on the sincerity and moral passion with which the orator spoke, not rhetorical polish and flair.

Rhetoricians have long regarded sincerity an important persuasive tool, and Roosevelt put great stock in this quality. "An orator would get a crowd," he said, "but he could not hold them if he lacked sincerity. If he isn't sincere, he has no business speaking." Moreover, "to admire the gift of oratory without regard to the moral quality behind the gift is to do wrong to the republic."[17] And it was this dimension of Roosevelt's delivery more than any other that moved his audiences.

When paired with his firm convictions on key issues, Roosevelt's oratory, while no match for the panache of a Lincoln or Reagan, was memorable. And of all Roosevelt's public speeches, none was more memorable, or important, than the Man with the Muck-Rake. With the Progressive, reformist mood sweeping the nation, Americans had no patience for philosophical platitudes or cute rhetoric. They demanded action. More specifically, citizens demanded action based on the fantastical, politically charged journalistic reporting they received in their daily newspapers and from influential writers of the time—some of whom were socialists—who sought to expose the excesses of industry and capitalism.

This is to say that the political climate was not terribly hospitable to Republicans. The GOP was viewed as being on the side of wealthy industrialists and the captains of commerce. Against this backdrop of yellow journalism and a national reformist sentiment, Roosevelt had the unenviable task of balancing Republican support of corporate interests on the one hand with citizens' demands for reforms of industries like the railroads and meatpacking on the other. For these reasons, Roosevelt's Man with the Muck-Rake speech not only laid claim to his title as a Progressive reformer but also, as Herbert Croly, the liberal founder of the *New Republic*, observed, may have saved the Republican Party from virtual extinction.[18]

Republicans have long battled liberal media bias. Historically, American newspapers were organs of political parties. While the dictum that one should never pick a fight with people who buy ink by the barrel (newspapers) or videotape by the mile (television) reigns supreme today, President Theodore Roosevelt was fearless in excoriating the yellow journalism of his era.

The Man with the Muck-Rake speech was delivered on April 15, 1906, at the laying of the cornerstone of the U.S. House of Representatives. A month prior, Roosevelt had tested his attack on irresponsible investigative journalists during a March 17 white-tie dinner of the Gridiron Club. By tradition, Gridiron Club events were confidential. This meant that the Washington elite who filled his erstwhile audience had been prevented from distributing or republishing his comments. Scholars debate whether Roosevelt intended his remarks to serve as a trial balloon to see how his remarks might be received. But on April 15 one thing was certain: Roosevelt's words ricocheted around the nation at warp speed.

The so-called man with the muck-rake was a reference to the figure from *Pilgrim's Progress*. As Roosevelt states in his speech, John Bunyan's man with the muck-rake "could look no way but downward, with the muck-rake in his hand; who was offered a celestial crown for his muck-rake, but who would neither look up nor regard the crown he was offered, but continued to rake to himself the filth of the floor." Roosevelt used the metaphor as a surrogate for all forms of sensational journalism and journalists. In a broader sense, his bromide was aimed at those who sought only to criticize and never to act. It wasn't that Roosevelt opposed a reporter's right to cover a story or to issue a strong critique; he had no problem with either of these. What incensed Roosevelt was the wild character assassinations and distortions promulgated by journalists who carped comfortably from the sidelines of leadership. His beef was with those who lacked the courage to enter the arena.

There is significant evidence that President Roosevelt had specific reporters, publishers, or papers in mind when he delivered his speech. First, when he delivered his earlier Gridiron Club address, the man with the muck-rake had likely been a reference to David Graham Phillips, a reporter for *Cosmopolitan*, whose scurrilous series "The Treason of the Senate" infuriated the president. Roosevelt's disdain for the publisher of *Cosmopolitan*, the infamous William Randolph Hearst, was also no secret.[19] Hearst, a Democrat, longed to become president of the United States. When he wasn't busy ordering his *New York Journal* employees to provide pictures so that he could spark the Spanish-American War, Hearst, who served in Congress, had his political operatives travel the nation lining up delegates for his 1904 run against Roosevelt. When Hearst tapped Phillips to write his screed against senators, of the twenty-one fingered, only three were Democrats. In a letter written to reporter Ray Stannard Baker before his speech, Roosevelt explained his rationale for delivering his address:

> One reason that I want to make that address is because . . . I feel that the man who in a yellow newspaper or in a yellow magazine . . . makes a ferocious attack on good men or even attacks bad men with exaggeration or for things they have not done, is a potent enemy of those of us who are really striving in good faith to expose bad men and drive them from power. I disapprove of the whitewash brush quite as much as of mudslinging, and it seems to me that the disapproval of one in no shape or way implies approval of the other. This I shall try to make clear.[20]

Roosevelt clearly had Hearst and his *Cosmopolitan* publication in mind: "These make-believe reformers, these preachers of rabid hatred, these ranters against corruption and in favor of social reform, these socialists who preach the creed of envy—in short, the people like those who write in the pages of the *Cosmopolitan*, are the real enemies of every effort to secure genuine reform, to secure social, civic, and political betterment." As journalism professor Mark Neuzil has suggested, Roosevelt's Man with the Muck-Rake speech can be viewed both as an indictment of the Hearst-style yellow journalism of the era and also as a way to curb Hearst's political ambitions.[21]

With books such as Upton Sinclair's *The Jungle* and Frank Norris's *The Octopus* attracting national acclaim and interest, President Roosevelt sought to secure for himself and the Republican Party a piece of the progressive reformist mantle. To have done otherwise, or to have ignored the impulses of the era, would have been politically ruinous for the Republican Party. The GOP was already viewed as being heavily on the side of powerful business interests. Roosevelt's critique of excessive wealth, while a departure from Republican discourse, functioned as a moderating influence that centered the GOP's image. Still, Roosevelt exhibited a fierce antipathy toward socialism. Here, then, is a truncated excerpt of the speech President Roosevelt delivered on April 15, 1906, that weaves together his attacks on the muckraking yellow journalists and that serves as a call for accurate reporting and virtuous living:

> *In "Pilgrim's Progress" the Man with the Muck-Rake is set forth as the example of him whose vision is fixed on carnal instead of on spiritual things. Yet he also typifies the man who in this life consistently refuses to see aught that is lofty, and fixes his eyes with solemn intentness only on that which is vile and debasing. Now, it is very necessary that we should not flinch from seeing what is vile and debasing. There is filth on the floor and it must be scraped up with the muck-rake; and there are times and places where this service is the most needed of all the services that can be performed. But the man who never does anything else, who never thinks or speaks or writes, save of his feats with the muck-rake, speedily becomes, not a help to society, not an incitement to good, but one of the most potent forces for evil. . . .*
>
> *Gross and reckless assaults on character, whether on the stump or in newspaper, magazine, or book, create a morbid and vicious public sentiment. . . .*
>
> *The men with the muck-rakes are often indispensable to the well-being of society; but only if they know when to stop raking the muck, and to look upward to the celestial crown above them, to the crown of worthy endeavor. . . .*
>
> *There are beautiful things above and roundabout them; and if they gradually grow to feel that the whole world is nothing but muck, their power of usefulness is gone. . . .*
>
> *At this moment we are passing through a period of great unrest—social, political, and industrial unrest. . . .*
>
> *Materially we must strive to secure a broader economic*

opportunity for all men, so that each shall have a better chance to show the stuff of which he is made. . . .

Spiritually and ethically we must strive to bring about clean living and right thinking. We appreciate also that the things of the soul are immeasurably more important. . . .

The foundation-stone of national life is, and ever must be, the high individual character of the average citizen.

News of President Roosevelt's Man with the Muck-Rake speech zipped around the globe and made headlines coast to coast and in Europe. Not surprisingly, Hearst's newspapers gave the speech negative treatment. Yet that didn't stop Hearst from finding a way to capitalize on Roosevelt's rough rhetoric against the muckraking yellow journalism for which the Hearst publications were famous. Hearst sold 450,000 copies of his "Treason of the Senate" series in the April 1906 issue of the *Cosmopolitan*.[22] The speech's wide acceptance by the broader public, however, put yellow journalists on notice.

Roosevelt's speech also drew criticism from some conservative Republicans who had recoiled at other portions of the speech that stated support for some type of progressive inheritance tax on the super rich. But as Lance Robinson notes in *American Conservatism: An Encyclopedia*, "Consistently progressive in public service, Roosevelt has nonetheless been appreciated by conservatives for his prudent foreign policy, unabashed nationalism, opposition to socialism and anarchism, and his forthright advocacy of individual virtue."[23] Likewise, Roosevelt biographer Edmund Morris argues that Roosevelt often toggled back and forth between sounding progressive themes and Republican ones.[24]

In an era arcing toward socialism, Roosevelt, like any powerful rhetorician, understood his audience and the limits imposed by the zeitgeist. But it had been his rhetorical dexterity, combined with a charismatic and sincere nature, that had produced a two-term presidency. Indeed, as several historians have noted, without Roosevelt's oratorical facility and populist instincts, the Republican Party might have faced electoral extinction.[25]

3

William F. Buckley Jr.

American Conservatism Finds Its Spokesman in the Speech That Wasn't

Yale Alumni Day Speech

FEBRUARY 1950 (UNDELIVERED)

YALE UNIVERSITY, NEW HAVEN, CONNECTICUT

---

*[National Review] stands athwart history, yelling Stop,
at a time when no one is inclined to do so, or to have much
patience with those who do.*

—William F. Buckley Jr. in the inaugural issue of *National Review*

William F. Buckley Jr.'s most influential speech may very well have been the one he chose not to deliver in February 1950. Admittedly, assigning a metric to the literally thousands of speeches the American conservative movement's greatest journalist and polemicist has delivered over his lifetime is difficult. Even after removing repeated deliveries of the same speech to different audiences (of which there are hundreds), Buckley's original speech texts number at least 184 and run 350,000 words in length. As Buckley once quipped, even *Gone with the Wind* contains only 250,000 words.

Buckley, a man without whom the Republican victories of the post–World War II era might never have been realized, has been called many things: "the godfather of American conservatism," "the architect of the modern conservative movement," and "the intellectual father of modern conservatism." President Ronald Reagan went even further: "Bill Buckley is perhaps the most influential journalist and intellectual in our era—he changed our country, indeed our century."

Yet whether Republicans know it or not, it was the speech that Buckley chose *not* to deliver in the Winter of 1950 that started it all.

William F. Buckley Jr., or WFB as his fans and associates often refer to him, was born a troublemaker and provocateur. When he was five years old, for example, Buckley had the perspicacity to write a letter to King George V arguing that His Majesty ought to repay Great Britain's overdue debts to the United States.[1] One of ten children, Buckley was born on November 24, 1925, in New York City. His parents were both devout Roman Catholics, his father a wealthy oil man. WFB is well known for his exacting command of English grammar and polysyllabic lexicon, but growing up on the family's estate in Sharon, Connecticut, Buckley's first language was the Spanish he learned from the family's Mexican nannies who mostly raised him. After graduating from Yale University in June 1950, Buckley returned three months later to teach an undergraduate course in Spanish. By 1944, he entered the army and had "a brief and bloodless experience in the Second World War" in the infantry and later as an administrative officer at Fort Sam Houston in San Antonio, Texas.[2] Later, he worked briefly for the Central Intelligence Agency and entertained a failed run to become the mayor of New York City, in which he received 13 percent of the vote. But it had been his decision in 1955 to found his magazine, *National Review*, that would have a profound and lasting impact on the Republican Party.

Republicans and conservatives talk about *National Review* using romantic language that, to the uninitiated, might sound strange: "You only have one first love," Claremont McKenna College government professor Charles Kesler says, "and mine (journalistically speaking) was *National Review*"; Edwin J. Feulner Jr., president of the Heritage Foundation, said that the first time he opened *National Review* "it opened my eyes to the network of people who thought like me"; "What has *NR* meant to me?" wrote Roger Kimball, coeditor of the *New Criterion*. "You might as well ask, What has the combination of sunshine and rain meant for those flowers in your backyard"; Colorado governor Bill Owens says that "*National Review* was for me not just a magazine but a complete political education"; and actor Tom Selleck says that *NR* emboldened him to stand strong in his conservative beliefs: "If a magazine as smart, funny, and factual as *National Review* could 'stand athwart history yelling Stop,' so could I."[3]

Selleck's quotation is a snippet of the oft-cited line from *National Review*'s 1955 inaugural issue wherein Buckley wrote that his conservative opinion journal, *National Review*, "stands athwart history, yelling Stop, at a time when no one is inclined to do so, or to have much patience with those who do." The magazine, which has never posted a financial profit, remains an essential gathering place for conservative Republican leaders. In its fifty-plus-year history, the fortnightly has waged numerous epic battles against both the left and the right. Of the latter, WFB is cited as having eliminated the John Birch Society, an ultra-rightwing group, from Republican ranks. The magazine often served as the glue that held the American conservative movement together. As Vice President Dick Cheney said, "It's no exaggeration to say that *NR* has had greater influence on the last half-century of human events than any other journal of opinion."[4]

But none of this would have been possible had it not been for the fracas over what was, at the time, Buckley's most prestigious public speaking invitation: the annual Yale University Alumni Day undergraduate oration. Buckley later said this experience more than anything else inspired him to write what became his first and best-selling book, *God and Man at Yale: The Superstitions of "Academic Freedom."* That's saying a lot; Buckley remains one of the most prolific conservative writers ever. As *Boston Globe* columnist Jeff Jacoby notes, WFB has written "35 nonfiction books, 15 books of fiction, 79 book reviews, 56 introductions or forewords to books written by others, 227 obituary essays, 800-plus editorials or other articles in *National Review*, 350 articles in periodicals other than *National Review*, and more than 4,000 newspaper columns."[5] In addition, in 1991 he was awarded the Presidential Medal of Freedom.

But it was the publication of *God and Man at Yale* that first ignited a young generation of conservatives and gave Buckley the national platform necessary to launch *National Review* and later his debate-style television show, *Firing Line*, which he hosted for more than thirty years—none of which might ever have happened had it not been for his decision to cancel a speech in February 1950.

No one delivers a speech quite like Buckley. The power of his oratory comes not from his physical presence but from the rich, stately, regal ring of his voice. Despite being born in New York City, Buckley is sometimes mistaken for being British. The curve to his accent is the result of having learned to speak English while attending day school in London. What's more, he has gained a reputation as being a Renaissance man: he is a lover of words and language, an avid snow skier and sailor, and has even mastered the harpsichord. His aura of cultured sophistication, combined with a crocodile grin, a sharp, protruding nose, and penetrating blue eyes, allow Buckley to project from the podium a level of supreme confidence, leavened with self-deprecation. In short, Buckley looks and sounds like a man who is always cocked and ready to fire off something profound. Seldom does he disappoint.

Therefore, it is hardly surprising that in December 1949, Buckley was selected as the undergraduate speaker for the annual February Alumni Day at Yale University. The honor was even greater than usual that year; Yale's graduating class of 1950 had entered with 1,800 students, 200 percent its normal size. "The class was greatly swollen because, ever since Pearl Harbor, Yale had grandly promised every graduating senior from high school whom it admitted using admissions' conventional criteria that when the war ended, by hook or by crook Yale would make room for him," said Buckley.[6] Even with the all-male student body's surge in enrollment (Yale didn't go co-ed until 1969), Buckley's intellectual, literary, and oratorical talents made him stand out. But it was his powerful articulation of atypical, he would say "freakishly conservative," political views that made his classmates and professors sit up and take notice.

According to Buckley, his conservative editorials as the head of the *Yale Daily News* raised the ire and interest of many students and professors:

I remember hearing about Professor Tom Mendenhall, who taught European history to a big class at Linsley-Chittenden. At a fellows' dinner in the spring of 1949 he regaled his colleagues with the story of his crashing disappointment that morning. "I had prepared a lecture centering on all the delinquencies of the Catholic Church in Europe, and after I was well launched on it, I looked up to feast on the expression on Buckley's face. But the son of a bitch wasn't there!"[7]

Still, Yale's administrators understood the value of a conservative rising star like Buckley. Yale's president at the time, Charles Seymour, once asked the dependably conservative WFB to submit clips of a half-dozen or so of his *Yale Daily News* editorials for him to show a potential Yale contributor. The prospective donor had asked Seymour to prove to him that "the place wasn't swarming with New Dealers." Buckley obliged.[8] But, as Seymour and others soon learned, WFB's decorum and gentlemanly manner were not signs of mindless obeisance. There were times, Buckley believed, when alumni should be forced to confront ideas and decisions larger than the sum of their next donation.

And that was precisely what young Buckley intended to do with his Alumni Day oration: force students, faculty, and the one thousand alumni scheduled to attend the event to confront the problems caused by a Yale University faculty packed with professors who were "collectivist in political and economic orientation, secular and humanistic in other studies."

In preparing for his high-profile debut before wealthy alumni donors, Buckley, a devout Catholic, had given thought to Yale's founding mission. He felt that the university had strayed from its founding values and was now, in fact, undermining them. As an undergraduate senior, he had to withstand four years of liberal teaching. He knew students at other universities were being forced to as well. Young Buckley believed this was a development worth not only noting but fighting. Thus, in the introductory portion of his speech draft, the brash twenty-four-year-old wrote:

I plan to unburden myself of one of the problems that is upper-most in my mind, as it must be in yours, and as it must be in the minds of all those men and women who contemplate the dilemma of mid-twentieth-century liberal American education. . . .

I defer to the seasoned and inquisitive and concerned alum-nus to help to solve this problem and to point out the way for Yale University. Yale was founded to educate young ministers for the Congregational Church. . . .

The nineteenth century served as the relaxing transition toward today, when the University seems to have no mission. . . .

This is what I want to know: Does not this policy of edu-cational laissez-faire imply that the standards and convictions of the president and fellows . . . are no better for Yale than those of any faculty member who devotes his energy and his time to proselytizing conflicting views? Does this mean that it is of no importance that President Seymour is a practicing Christian and Professor Smith is a professional anti-Christian, because Pres-ident Seymour's opinion on this subject is no more valid than Professor Smith's?

Buckley's opening salvo is both powerful and prescient. By begin-ning with Yale's historical origins, the young conservative had both reflected his dedication to tradition and connected with his older audience, a group whose age placed them closer to Yale's origins. WFB forewent the temptation to switch into an ideological rant. Instead, he advanced an artful argument designed to pulverize the early ideological pillars of what would later become known as "moral-philosophical relativism"—the notion that there is no such thing as good and bad, right and wrong; rather, all views are relative to those who espouse them, and therefore all are equally valued. Not only was moral relativism a departure from Yale's founding, Buckley argued, but such a position if allowed to continue would turn in on itself to destroy the university's original mission of spreading Christ-ian doctrine and belief.

Buckley also personalized his critique by identifying not only Yale's president but also the concepts and philosophies held and taught by the university's professors. Like any good rhetorician must, Buckley then anticipated and addressed the possible objections of his audience:

> But the case is overstated, you will say. After all, didn't President Seymour last spring state that he would not knowingly appoint a Communist to the faculty? Most certainly he did. (It is interesting, too, that his assertion was considered audacious.) But against what did the president rule? Against an extreme extreme. He might with equal daring have ruled against student polygamy. What steps is the administration allowed to take to show up socialism, the blood-brother of Marxism? What steps are taken to rule out polygamy as a moral, rather than a merely sociological evil? Certainly these questions are rhetorical, because so long as Yale professes this uncurbed, all-encompassing, fanatical allegiance to laissez-faire education she will lead her students nowhere. [Yale will not reaffirm its standards] because to do so would bring from the liberals the cry of educational totalitarianism, and Yale is very, very allergic to criticism from the liberal, who is the absolute dictator in the United States today.

What had begun as a critique in this passage turns into a bromide. Buckley wasn't just arguing for a return to Yale's Christian traditions. No, the twenty-four-year-old Buckley intended to argue for a return to moral standards and absolutes. It was from this seed that the rhetorical roots of the conservative oratorical style blossomed. If one accepts that there is such a thing as right and wrong, good and evil, then one must correspondingly believe that students should be taught a curriculum that reflects this fact. To do otherwise "will lead students nowhere." Thus, to assume a posture of "laissez-faire education," as Buckley calls it, betrays Yale's mission and absolute Truth with it.

The dilemma is frightening. Suppose the administration of Yale were to formulate in unambiguous terms its educational credo. Suppose this credo were to assert that Yale considers active Christianity the first basis of enlightened thought and action. Suppose it reasserted its belief in democracy. Suppose it asserted that it considered Communism, socialism, collectivism, government paternalism inimical to the dignity of the individual and to the strength and prosperity of the nation, save where the government and only the government could act in the interests of humanitarianism and national security. Suppose Yale were to go on to say that whereas every student must recognize and explore conflicting views and of course ultimately formulate for himself his own credo, nevertheless the University would not sustain prominent members of the faculty who sought to violate the explicit purpose of this University by preaching *doctrines against which the officials of the University had cast judgment.*

By offering a series of parallel repetitions, Buckley's string of hypothetical university sanctions served to startle and alarm older alumni. In their day, a Yale education would have no need to reaffirm such basic and elemental tenets as the belief that God is the spring from which enlightenment flows, that democracy is good, and that Communism is bad. This was a "frightening" development, Buckley planned to say. With World War II behind them and the Korean War looming on the horizon, Buckley's message would likely have packed a persuasive punch. He was in essence arguing that everything the United States and the Allies had fought and died for—the defense of Christianity against atheist domination and the triumph of democracy over Communism—was being destroyed, not on the battlefield, but in the university classroom—and of their alma mater, no less.

The Republican Party's long-standing anti-Communist posture features prominently in Buckley's speech. As was seen in the examination of Abraham Lincoln, and as will be seen in other speeches, the Republican Party's traditionalist values have, more so than Democratic oratory, embraced and exhibited a strong Judeo-Christian tenor marked by policies that value faith over secularism. Therefore, sounding these themes in a speech to alumni who attended a university built to educate ministers would not only be in keeping with Buckley's pro–Judeo-Christian views but it would also sound the alarm that Yale's traditions were eroding and in retreat. WFB's next passage further stokes the anxieties he ignited by arguing that the beliefs of faculty and the beliefs of alumni are now engaged in an invisible war:

> *There would come a great hue and cry. A hundred organizations would lash out against Yale. They would accuse her of traducing education, of violating freedom. These charges would be loud, pointed, violent, and superficial—superficial because Yale is a private institution and acknowledges responsibility to her alumni, her community and herself. . . . Her faculty must hold certain opinions. Why not opinions that, in general, tally with those of the trustees of the institution, and that hold, with the trustees, a common goal?*

Here, Buckley, the self-proclaimed troublemaker, can be seen in full relief. This passage is the equivalent of rhetorical fuel dumped on a flame. Buckley intended to taunt and dare alumni to reassert their authority and leadership by guarding their beloved institution's legacy. In doing so, he knocked down concerns over a possible faculty uproar by reminding the one thousand alumni (many of whom represented the financial gears of the institution) that Yale's status as a private institution gave them every right to weigh in on such matters. Buckley planned to conclude his February 1950 Alumni Day Oration as follows:

> *And so we saw in eighteenth-century Yale a thesis in education. Two hundred and fifty years later we see the antithesis, and perhaps the time has come to resolve the two and proceed to the synthesis: the modern, free, enlightened University with a*

purpose, and with the will, the courage, and the conviction to imbue her students with that same purpose. This is a purpose which you and I and presumably the officers of Yale consider magnificent and noble. It is certainly their right to desire and to insist that in so far as it is possible this purpose be passed on to succeeding generations—at least to that portion of succeeding generations that is processed by Yale.

After writing his speech, protocol for Alumni Day orators dictated that Buckley submit his final speech draft to the Yale News Bureau. When he did so just forty-eight hours before he was to deliver the speech, Buckley says he remembers the exact words the director of the bureau, Yale press secretary Dick Lee, said to him as he handed Lee his speech draft: "What are you saying in it? Nothing, I hope!"

Within two hours of Buckley's submission, a senior officer of the alumni hierarchy walked across campus to tell WFB that President Seymour had been "deeply disappointed" with his proposed speech and that the secretary of the university thought the address "an indictment of the administration" and wanted to know whether Buckley would consider revising his remarks. The official told Buckley that "the alumni simply wouldn't *understand* it . . . they'll leave the place thinking Yale is communistic . . . the alumni can't grasp your point."

The gentleman and stalwart in Buckley responded: He would clarify any portions of "alumni misunderstanding," but the rest would stay; his message would be a dart, not a laurel. Buckley then graciously added that if the administrators felt strongly enough that his speech was not in the best interests of Yale, he would withdraw himself from the program.[9] "At first, my offers to withdraw were met with hurt feelings and with astonishment at my even having considered this solution," he wrote. "The University had conferred upon me an honor, and it would certainly not be revoked—besides which, it was too late to get a substitute. I offered not only to secure a substitute, but to write him a speech of the 'good old Yale' variety, but this offer was also spurned."[10] President Seymour responded that, regrettably, WFB's offer to withdraw was accepted.

. . .

In the aftermath of his never-delivered Yale Alumni Day oration fiasco, with some reservation the Yale Class Council later asked Buckley to deliver the Class Day oration on, June 11, 1950. That important speech contained similar if muted themes, and it was Buckley's most visible public speaking venue before leaving Yale. But the Alumni Day conflagration had roused the provocateur in Buckley. If Yale's administration didn't like Buckley's oral critique, how would they like a book-length treatise preserved in printed form for all alumni to read for years to come? he wondered. Thus the seed was sown for what became Buckley's first and most well-known book, *God and Man at Yale: The Superstitions of "Academic Freedom."*

The book's short- and long-term effects on the American conservative movement, and by extension the GOP, were immense. *God and Man at Yale* became a conservative classic that inspired a young breed of college conservatives who soon found their presidential spokesman in Barry Goldwater and later in Ronald Reagan. What's more, with *God and Man at Yale* launching Buckley's meteoric rise to the top of the literary, political, and scholarly worlds, the twenty-five-year-old author had instantly created a national platform upon which to build future efforts, most notably *National Review.*

But from the start, Buckley says the thing that sparked the idea for *God and Man at Yale* had been the bitter rejection of the Alumni Day speech he never delivered. Asked what prompted him to write *God and Man at Yale*, Buckley said:

The catalyst was the annual Alumni Day event in February of my senior year. There was always an undergraduate speaker, and in 1950 I was selected. . . . There was great static—the event was scheduled for Saturday—so I sent a message to Mr. Seymour offering to withdraw as speaker; offer accepted. But the ideas that I had explored in that speech took root. I graduated, got married that July, and took on the book. . . . It came out just as Yale was celebrating its 250th birthday, and much indignation was worked up to the effect that I had all along planned to subvert Yale's celebration, which was on the order of saying that a baby born on Christmas Day was designed, last March, to get in the way of festivities.[11]

A man of William F. Buckley Jr.'s towering intellect and eloquence was undoubtedly headed for shining shores. But in his senior-year scuffle with Yale's administrators over his scheduled February 1950 Alumni Day oration, the concept for the first of Buckley's dozens of books had been born. The themes of his never-delivered speech presaged the broadsides he later unloaded in *God and Man at Yale*; namely, that the moral and religious virtues of our ancestors are worth preserving and that universities must never become the breeding grounds for monolithic leftist indoctrination. Rather, higher education should foster true intellectual diversity, and democracy's triumph over Marxist visions must not only occur militarily, but educationally as well.

As was discussed in the introduction, this is a battle that rages on even today, fifty-five years after Buckley fired the opening shot. But Buckley had the courage and intellect to shoot first. And in so doing, he set in motion a literary career that has emboldened millions of conservative foot soldiers to keep firing back.

4

Dwight D. Eisenhower

Strategic Speechifying

Atoms for Peace

DECEMBER 8, 1953

UNITED NATIONS GENERAL ASSEMBLY, NEW YORK, NEW YORK

So my country's purpose is to help us move out of the dark chamber of horrors into the light, to find a way by which the minds of men, the hopes of men, the souls of men everywhere, can move forward toward peace and happiness and well-being.

-—Dwight D. Eisenhower

Dwight David Eisenhower personified America. He was a product of the midwestern wide open spaces—strong, active, and creative. He loved to paint, played football at West Point, and had a smile that radiated America's warm and welcoming nature. To outsiders, it was easy to dismiss Eisenhower as a kind but unthinking jock-turned-military man, a simpleton, as further evidence that the United States was little more than a shallow nation that lacked intellectual seriousness. But just as America's foes would realize the strength of U.S. resolve, so, too, would Ike's international and domestic critics learn that behind that grandfatherly warmth and winning smile lay a strategic thinker and speaker. As Princeton University professor of politics Fred I. Greenstein's acclaimed treatise on Eisenhower later revealed, Ike had been the master strategist of a "hidden-hand presidency" that employed words as weapons to keep the peace.[1]

Throughout history, Republicans have long benefited from being underestimated. During presidential campaigns, Democrats have had an impressive record of taking the bait by casting Republicans as intellectually inferior: Abraham Lincoln was a rail-splitting dolt; Ike was a dumb military man and former football player who was an inarticulate deliverer of jumbled syntax; Ronald Reagan was a hollow simpleton and Hollywood actor; George W. Bush is a frat boy and intellectual lightweight; on and on it goes. But Democrats' love affair with intellectualism (some would say pseudointellectualism), and the attending echoes of elitism that emanate from a political philosophy that gives federal bureaucrats greater control over individuals, has often been Republicans' secret weapon. American audiences are not European audiences. Americans love an underdog. But more than that, they love someone who is comfortable enough in his own skin and who doesn't feel the need to flaunt his intelligence.

On June 6, 1944, as supreme commander of the Allied Expeditionary Force during World War II, then general Dwight D. Eisenhower directed the largest ever amphibious assault in military history, the legendary D day invasion of Normandy. Eisenhower biographer Geoffrey Perret notes that this experience "had a transforming effect on his already outgoing personality and shrewd, probing mind. . . . When a man has that much power, the trappings of authority are almost irrelevant."[2]

In the wake of World War II, Eisenhower's enormous national popularity meant that he didn't need to try to impress. Both Democrats and Republicans urged him to run for president. Eisenhower's presence and inner reservoir of self-confidence carried with it a supreme authority, a quiet command, that was obvious to all. Indeed, from the country's founding, Americans have tapped generals to become their presidents. Beginning with George Washington, Americans have held a belief that the attributes of leadership, devotion, sacrifice, and management endemic to the battlefield are transferable to the duties of the chief executive.

But commanding men on the battlefield had instilled in Eisenhower a respect for war's horrors as well as its effectiveness in achieving historic change. He had also learned that while clear and direct communication was essential, obfuscation and indirection were potent psychological weapons against an enemy. Eisenhower's communicative application of both of these principles yielded historic dividends.

An early instance occurred in his Atoms for Peace address to the United Nations General Assembly in New York City on December 8, 1953. Months before Eisenhower's historic speech, the top-secret Oppenheimer Report had stressed the dire need to promote wider public discussion and understanding of the stakes involved in a possible nuclear Armageddon. Specifically, the report had called for galvanizing public opinion behind a foreign policy that could avert another global war. The challenge, of course, was how best to initiate such a discussion without sparking panic among citizens or, worse, members of the international community. Delivering a hard-hitting frontal attack against the Soviet Union was not in keeping with Eisenhower's strategy for combatting Soviet expansionism. Although fiercely anti-Communist, the president's moderate pragmatism required that any major speech be couched in the language of peace, even if its subtext involved warning the Soviets of the consequences of a war with the United States.

Martin J. Medhurst, arguably the nation's foremost expert on Dwight D. Eisenhower's rhetoric, states that "Eisenhower's 'Atoms for Peace' speech was, in fact, a carefully-crafted piece of cold war rhetoric specifically designed to gain a 'psychological' victory over the Soviet Union" that served "partly as warning, partly as challenge."[3] Eisenhower aide C. D. Jackson and Admiral Lewis L. Strauss, chairman of the Atomic Energy Commission, were the primary writers of the speech. Jackson and Lewis wrote eleven drafts before arriving at the final version Eisenhower delivered on December 8, 1953, to the United Nations at 2:45 p.m.

On his way toward setting up his psychological war message, President Eisenhower unfurled a message of cooperation, peacefulness, and hope. The word *peace* had been a mainstay of Eisenhower's presidential campaigns. Advertising guru Rosser Reeves had even imbedded the word in the general's campaign slogan: "Eisenhower, Man of Peace."[4] This tagline artfully inoculated Ike from taking on an image of bellicosity. In Atoms for Peace, Eisenhower invoked the word *peace* or one of its variants (for example, *peaceful*) twenty-six times. And in the opening paragraphs of his address, the word *hope* was used five times. As religious studies scholar Ira Chernus observed, Eisenhower "had to use the word peace as a weapon of cold war."[5]

After establishing a hopeful, peace-seeking tone of conciliation, the president's speech took an abrupt turn toward the ominous stakes of atomic warfare:

> *I feel impelled to speak today in a language that in a sense is new, one which I, who have spent so much of my life in the military profession, would have preferred never to use. That new language is the language of atomic warfare. . . . On July 16, 1945, the United States set off the world's first atomic explosion. Since that date in 1945, the United States of America has conducted forty-two test explosions. Atomic bombs today are more than twenty-five times as powerful as the weapons with which the atomic age dawned, while hydrogen weapons are in the ranges of millions of tons of TNT equivalent. Today, the United States' stockpile of atomic weapons, which, of course, increases daily, exceeds by many times the total [explosive] equivalent of the total of all bombs and all shells that came from every plane and every gun in every theatre of war in all the years of World War II. A single air group, whether afloat or land based, can now deliver to any reachable target a destructive cargo exceeding in power all the bombs that fell on Britain in all of World War II. In the United States, the Army, the Navy, the Air Force, and the Marine Corps are all capable of putting this weapon to military use.*

Under the guise of a recitation of facts, Eisenhower's opening salvo reminded the world in general, and the Soviet Union in particular, of the stakes involved in any provocation of the United States. By reminding his listeners that he had spent the majority of his life in military leadership positions, Eisenhower used his "hidden-hand" rhetoric to implicitly state that U.S. forces were armed to the hilt and under the direction of a general who was prepared to destroy any enemy who dared to attack the United States. This strategy of saying something without saying it recurs throughout his address:

> Should such an atomic attack be launched against the United States, our reactions would be swift and resolute. But for me to say that the defense capabilities of the United States are such that they could inflict terrible losses upon an aggressor, for me to say that the retaliation capabilities of the United States are so great that such an aggressor's land would be laid waste, all this, while fact, is not the true expression of the purpose and the hope of the United States.
>
> To pause there would be to confirm the hopeless finality of a belief that two atomic colossi are doomed malevolently to eye each other indefinitely across a trembling world. To stop there would be to accept helplessly the probability of civilization destroyed, the annihilation of the irreplaceable heritage of mankind handed down to us generation from generation, and the condemnation of mankind to begin all over again the age-old struggle upward from savagery toward decency, and right, and justice. Surely no sane member of the human race could discover victory in such desolation.

The opening paragraph of this passage is a classic example of what rhetoricians call affirmation by denial. That is, by a speaker saying he or she wishes *not* to express a sentiment, he or she expresses exactly that sentiment. Thus, by stating that it was not the president's purpose to suggest that the United States would unleash nuclear hell on a Soviet attack, President Eisenhower was in effect making this very point.

The second paragraph of this critical passage casts the Soviet-American standoff in the darkest of terms. The image he paints is one where two nuclear superpowers are gripped by perennial fear marked by "doom" and "trembling," an image desirable to neither side. In a diary entry penned two days after his speech, Eisenhower wrote that underlying his Atoms for Peace address had been "the clear conviction that as of now the world is racing toward catastrophe—that something must be done to put a brake on this movement." He understood that words alone could not avert calamity, but the president wrote that he believed "ideas expressed in words must certainly have a function in getting people . . . to devise ways and means by which the possible disaster of the future can be avoided."[6]

> *Could anyone wish his name to be coupled by history with such human degradation and destruction? Occasional pages of history do record the faces of the "great destroyers," but the whole book of history reveals mankind's never-ending quest for peace and mankind's God-given capacity to build. It is with the book of history, and not with isolated pages, that the United States will ever wish to be identified. My country wants to be constructive, not destructive. It wants agreements, not wars, among nations. It wants itself to live in freedom and in the confidence that the people of every other nation enjoy equally the right of choosing their own way of life. So my country's purpose is to help us move out of the dark chamber of horrors into the light, to find a way by which the minds of men, the hopes of men, the souls of men everywhere, can move forward toward peace and happiness and well-being.*

This passage was key. In it, the president had rhetorically defined any individual or nation willing to accept the status quo and its inevitable horrors as outside the pale of respectable international standing. Eisenhower had thrown down the gauntlet of international public opinion. Yet instead of issuing a militaristic challenge, the former general backed the Soviets into a rhetorical corner that challenged them to match his peaceful gesture, fissionable unit for fissionable unit:

We never have, we never will, propose or suggest that the Soviet Union surrender what is rightfully theirs. We will never say that the people of Russia are an enemy with whom we have no desire ever to deal or mingle in friendly and fruitful relationship. . . . I therefore make the following proposals:

The governments principally involved, to the extent permitted by elementary prudence, to begin now and continue to make joint contributions from their stockpiles of normal uranium and fissionable materials to an international atomic energy agency. . . . Experts would be mobilized to apply atomic energy to the needs of agriculture, medicine, and other peaceful activities. A special purpose would be to provide abundant electrical energy in the power-starved areas of the world. Thus the contributing Powers would be dedicating some of their strength to serve the needs rather than the fears of mankind. . . .

Of those "principally involved" the Soviet Union must, of course, be one. I would be prepared to submit to the Congress of the United States, and with every expectation of approval, any such plan that would, first, encourage world-wide investigation into the most effective peacetime uses of fissionable material, and with the certainty that they [the investigators] had all the material needed for the conduct of all experiments that were appropriate; second, begin to diminish the potential destructive power of the world's atomic stockpiles; third, allow all peoples of all nations to see that, in this enlightened age, the great Powers of the earth, both of the East and of the West, are interested in human aspirations first rather than in building up the armaments of war; fourth, open up a new channel for peaceful discussion and initiate at least a new approach to the many difficult problems that must be solved in both private and public conversations, if the world is to shake off the inertia imposed by fear and is to make positive progress toward peace.

Against the dark background of the atomic bomb, the United States does not wish merely to present strength, but also the desire and the hope for peace. The coming months will be fraught with fateful decisions. In this Assembly, in the capitals and military headquarters of the world, in the hearts of men everywhere, be they governed or governors, may they be the decisions which will lead this world out of fear and into peace.

President Eisenhower's speech had coaxed cooperation as a way to engage the Soviet Union through public, not military, pressure. As part of his "New Look" strategy, Eisenhower believed that Atoms for Peace would (1) show smaller nations that atomic energy could serve their needs and interests, (2) encourage Americans that the vast financial resources their government had poured into atomic research was not without positive, hopeful uses, and (3) that even if the Soviet Union was to go along with the creation of the International Atomic Energy Agency for "propaganda purposes," "the United States could afford to reduce its atomic stockpile by two or three times the amount the Russians might contribute, and still improve our relative position."[7]

Fred Greenstein calls Atoms for Peace "one of the rhetorical landmarks of Eisenhower's eight years in office." Indeed, when Gallup took its soundings following President Eisenhower's address, Ike's approval rating had jumped eight points to a commanding 66 percent national approval rating, with only 20 percent disapproval. Critics would contend that Ike had raised international expectations for world peace to unrealistically high levels. But the president's strategy had staunched Communism and opened up new pathways for peaceful Soviet engagement.

As Eisenhower scholar Martin J. Medhurst wrote, in this way, "Eisenhower was able to accomplish his goals. He warned the Soviet Union against a preemptive strike; he portrayed the United States as the friend and benefactor of the developing world; and, most importantly, he placed the Soviet Union in a policy dilemma by challenging the U.S.S.R to accept his atoms-for-peace proposal."[8] Indeed, the World War II warrior who had so masterfully led Americans as they stormed the beaches at Normandy had now opened up another beachhead, one of negotiation and pressure.

"Little Rock"

SEPTEMBER 24, 1957

OVAL OFFICE, THE WHITE HOUSE, WASHINGTON, D.C.

———————

Mob rule cannot be allowed to override the decisions of our
courts. . . . Our enemies are gloating over this incident and
using it everywhere to misrepresent our whole nation.

—Dwight D. Eisenhower

If President Eisenhower possessed any major flaw, it was that he held too optimistic a view of human nature to find within itself the courage to do what was morally right. During a July 17, 1957, press conference, a reporter had reminded Eisenhower that executive authority included the right to use force to ensure that schools were integrated. The president acknowledged that he had this power, but added, "I can't imagine any set of circumstances that would ever induce me to send federal troops . . . into an area to enforce the orders of a federal court. . . . The common sense of Americans will never require it."[9]

Eisenhower's aversion to federal intervention was the result of both his Republican philosophy of limited executive power and his reluctance to use military troops to intervene in domestic affairs. As only a soldier can, President Eisenhower respected the awesome and awful power a military presence could command. He believed deeply in the importance of restraint. And, like most Republicans, he believed that while government can change the shape of the law, no law can change the shape of an individual's heart. As he said during a press conference on the morning the news out of Little Rock, Arkansas, broke, "You cannot change people's hearts merely by laws."[10]

The Republican Party had been battling the forces of slavery and African American oppression from its founding; the issue was in large measure the catalyst for the creation of the GOP. But Eisenhower's faith that individuals would stand on the right side of history soon proved overly optimistic. He underestimated the determination of Arkansas's Democratic governor, Orval E. Faubus, the White Citizens Councils, and the nearly 250,000 Faubus supporters to ban black children from attending Little Rock's Central High School.

On September 2, 1957, in response to the *Brown* decision to integrate public schools, Faubus, a man the *New York Times* referred to as "a Democrat with a liberal background," sent 270 armed National Guardsmen and 50 state police to Central High School in Little Rock to ensure that 9 black children were prevented from attending school.[11] That evening, Faubus delivered a televised address to the people of Arkansas:

> A federal court has ruled that no further litigation is possible before the forcible integration of Negroes and whites in Central High School tomorrow, the evidence of discord, anger and resentment has come to me from so many sources as to become a deluge. . . . [Little Rock is] on the brink of a riot while outraged white mothers . . . prepared to march on the school at 6 a.m.; caravans of indignant white citizens . . . converg[ed] on Little Rock from all over Arkansas. And Little Rock stores . . . were selling out of knives.[12]

With the federal courts scheduled to confer on the legality of Governor Faubus's intervention just two and a half weeks later, President Eisenhower exercised restraint. Surely, Eisenhower reasoned, Faubus would come to his senses and obey federal court orders. On September 14, the president met with Faubus in a small office at the Newport News naval base. The Arkansas governor tried to woo Eisenhower by recounting his wartime service and by reiterating that he had nothing but the highest respect for the law. The guardsmen, Faubus assured Eisenhower, were only there to maintain order. Eisenhower bought it; the president agreed to allow the troops to maintain order until such time as the black students could enroll.[13]

During the interim, however, Faubus and his supporters had grown in both intensity and number. Mobs had gathered outside Central High and were determined to keep the nine black students from entering the school. "Two! Four! Six! Eight! We ain't gonna integrate!" they chanted.[14]

The nine black students were let into Central High through a side door to be enrolled. The mob on the street erupted. "The ni——rs are in our school," the mob yelled as they rushed police lines. "Lynch the ni——rs!" yelled the rioters.[15] Within twenty-four hours, President Eisenhower received a telegram from Woodrow Wilson Mann, the mayor of Little Rock: IMMEDIATE NEED FOR FEDERAL TROOPS IS URGENT. . . . PEOPLE ARE CONVERGING ON THE SCHOOL FROM ALL DIRECTIONS. . . . MOB IS ARMED . . . SITUATION IS OUT OF CONTROL.[16]

The telegram read like something the former general might have received from a besieged army unit during World War II. Faubus's forces of bigotry had proved too much to hold back. The general-turned-president deployed a thousand paratroopers from the 101st Airborne Division to tamp down violence and uphold the law. Only in extreme instances did Republicans believe military forces should be used on U.S. soil. Yet, the fulfillment of the law demanded it. On September 24, 1957, President Eisenhower spoke to the American people to explain his decision to act:

> I want to speak to you about the serious situation that has arisen in Little Rock. . . . Disorderly mobs have deliberately prevented the carrying out of proper orders from a Federal Court. Local authorities have not eliminated that violent opposition and, under the law, I yesterday issued a Proclamation calling upon the mob to disperse. This morning the mob again gathered

in front of the Central High School of Little Rock, obviously for the purpose of again preventing the carrying out of the Court's order relating to the admission of Negro children to that school. . . . I have today issued an Executive Order directing the use of troops under Federal authority to aid in the execution of Federal law at Little Rock, Arkansas. . . . The interest of the nation in the proper fulfillment of the law's requirements cannot yield to opposition and demonstrations by some few persons. Mob rule cannot be allowed to override the decisions of our courts.

Now, let me make it very clear that Federal troops are not being used to relieve local and state authorities of their primary duty to preserve the peace and order of the community. . . . The running of our school system and the maintenance of peace and order in each of our States are strictly local affairs and the Federal Government does not interfere except in a very few special cases.

Eisenhower walked the line between respecting states' rights and upholding federal enforcement "in a very few special cases." This, the president argued, was one such case. By reiterating adherence to the law as his guiding principle, Eisenhower remained on firm rhetorical ground with law-and-order Republicans. Still, as he makes clear in his next passage, Eisenhower explained that his decision should not be interpreted as a blight on the South, but as an action against a select "mob" of individuals.

I have deemed it a great personal privilege to spend in our Southland tours of duty while in the military service and enjoyable recreational periods since that time. So from intimate personal knowledge, I know that the overwhelming majority of the people in the South including those of Arkansas and of Little Rock are of good will, united in their efforts to preserve and respect the law even when they disagree with it. They do not sympathize with mob rule. They, like the rest of our nation, have proved in two great wars their readiness to sacrifice for America. A foundation of our American way of life is our national respect for law. In the South, as elsewhere, citizens are keenly aware of the tremendous disservice that has been done to the people of Arkansas in the eyes of the nation, and that has been done to the nation in the eyes of the world.

In a way that only he could, the hero general saved face for the South by personalizing both his experiences in the South and the blood he had witnessed southern men spill in battle for their nation. His reasons for doing so were, in one sense, political. After all, at the time the GOP was hardly viable in what was then the Democratic "solid South." Republicans had long desired to make inroads with southern voters. As someone who had commanded southern soldiers, Eisenhower was uniquely aware of how sensitivity over southern pride might be interpreted. Thus, his line reminding Americans that southerners had "proved in two great wars their readiness to sacrifice for America" was a subtle, yet deft, invocation of the Lincolnian rhetoric of conciliation and post–Civil War healing. In essence, the president was telling the nation, "I fought with men from the South. They're good people. Don't let stereotypes about 'racist southerners' cloud your judgment. The mob doesn't speak for the majority." With the South's patriotism safeguarded and decoupled from the actions of the racist mob, Eisenhower was free to lower the hammer on those individuals whose actions had triggered him to deploy federal troops to Little Rock:

At a time when we face grave situations abroad because of the hatred that Communism bears toward a system of government based on human rights, it would be difficult to exaggerate the harm that is being done to the prestige and influence, and indeed to the safety, of our nation and the world. Our enemies are gloating over this incident and using it everywhere to misrepresent our whole nation.

This was about as close as a president can come to calling citizens "traitors" or "Communist sympathizers" and still get away with it. He had shamed the rioters as people who were aiding the cause of Communism. And in doing so, the president had returned to the well from whence his popularity flowed: standing firm in the face of Communist aggression and tyranny, a cause behind which the overwhelming majority of Americans could unite. Moreover, because he had stood across the battlefield from tyrannical regimes, President Eisenhower effectively silenced his political detractors. Put another way, Ike's very presence conveyed a sense of authority and respect that could only come through having rendered historic military service.

The paratroopers from the 101st Airborne Division remained in place for a year and were forced to thwart five attempts to bomb Little Rock Central High School. In 1958, Governor Faubus was reelected. The nine African American students who had risked their lives for an education eventually graduated from high school and attended college. President Eisenhower had, like the Republican leaders before him, struck a blow against black oppression. As he once told an associate following the first *Brown* decision, "I suppose nobody knows how they [African Americans] feel or how many pressures or insults they have to take. I guess the only way you can realize exactly how they feel is to have a black skin for a few weeks."[17]

Before leaving office, President Eisenhower signed into law both the 1957 and 1960 Civil Rights Acts. As rhetoric scholars Steven R. Goldzwig and George N. Dionisopoulos concluded, "By sending federal troops to Little Rock to protect the equal rights of children to attend school, Eisenhower became a key participant in helping restore a political, historical, and cultural vision of a nation and a republicanism represented by one of his most esteemed predecessors, Abraham Lincoln."[18] President Eisenhower's strong speech supporting the rule of law marshalled the right words for the right side of history.

5

Everett Dirksen

The Speech That Made the Civil Rights Act of 1964 Possible

"The Time Has Come"

I appeal to all senators. We are confronted with a moral issue. Today let us not be found wanting in whatever it takes by way of moral and spiritual substance to face up to the issue and to vote cloture.

—Everett Dirksen

It is hard to overstate the consistency and ferocity with which Democrats throughout U.S. history have opposed civil rights legislation and protections for African Americans. As black PBS television commentator Tony Brown wrote, "It is out of ignorance of their own history that many Blacks demean the Republican philosophy and condemn Black Republicans. Blacks have been Republicans historically. . . . Democrats working hand in hand with the Ku Klux Klan gave us Jim Crow Laws that effectively enslaved Blacks."[1] Indeed, the GOP has been responsible for ensuring the passage of virtually every single major civil rights initiative in U.S. history, including winning passage of the Thirteenth, Fourteenth, and Fifteenth Amendments, and the Civil Rights Act of 1957, and authoring, introducing, and seeing to passage the 1960 Civil Rights Act. But it would be a speech by Everett McKinley Dirksen, the Republican Senate minority leader, leading his small band of Senate Republicans, that would pave the way for yet *another* civil rights victory: the Civil Rights Act of 1964.

On June 10, 1964, at exactly 9:51 a.m., Senator Robert C. Byrd, the Democrat from West Virginia, spoke the last word of what had been a fourteen-hour-and-thirteen-minute-long speech. The Democratic senator, who continues to serve even today, is revered by members of the Democratic Party. Former Democratic Senate leader Tom Daschle says that "Robert C. Byrd is truly a legend in his own time. He stands larger than life, not only for his accomplishments, but also for his principles."[2] Indeed, Byrd holds the distinction of having served in more leadership positions than any member of either party in Senate history. Massachusetts senator Ted Kennedy has praised Byrd as personifying "what our Founding Fathers were thinking about when they were thinking about a United States Senate. He brings the kind of qualities that the Founding Fathers believed were so important for service to the Nation."[3] And it was the weight of all Byrd's experience and his deep knowledge of Senate rules that the premiere leader of the Democratic Party would put to use in leading a filibuster to kill the landmark Civil Rights Act of 1964.

A former grand dragon of the Ku Klux Klan (KKK), Senator Byrd was selected by his fellow Democrats to serve as Senate Democratic whip in 1971. In 1977, his Democratic colleagues elected him Democratic leader, a position he held for six consecutive terms. For an impressive twelve years, the former Klansman held the position of Democratic leader—from January 1977 through December 1988—and served as Democratic majority leader six years (1977–1980, 1987–1988) and as Senate minority leader six years (1981–1986).

Byrd's views toward African Americans are both shameful and well documented. Three years after the Democratic senator claimed to have ended his membership in the KKK, in a letter to the imperial Wizard of the KKK, Byrd wrote that "[t]he Klan is needed today as never before and I am anxious to see its rebirth here in West Virginia . . . and in every state in the Union."[4] Desegregation of the armed forces had also angered Byrd. In another letter written after his alleged exit from the KKK, Byrd stated that he would never fight "with a Negro by my side. Rather I should die a thousand times, and see Old Glory trampled in the dirt never to rise again, than to see this beloved land of ours become degraded by race mongrels, a throwback to the blackest specimen from the wilds."[5] And as recently as 2001, Byrd shocked FOX News viewers when the West Virginia Democrat had this to say during a live interview with then host Tony Snow: "There are white ni——rs. I've seen a lot of white ni——rs in my time. I'm going to use that word. We just need to work together to make our country a better country, and I'd just as soon quit talking about it so much."[6] But in 1964, Senator Byrd, along with over one-third of Senate Democrats, and ninety-six House Democrats, had their sights set on one thing: killing the Civil Rights Act.

In 1963, President John F. Kennedy sent a civil rights bill to Congress, the elements of which would eventually form the Civil Rights Act of 1964. The bill created a rift between the southern and northern elements of the Democratic Party. Both Kennedy and Vice President Lyndon Baines Johnson worried that the defeat of civil rights legislation would create an intraparty fissure capable of threatening their political futures. Thus, on learning of African American civil rights leaders' desire to generate support for the bill by holding a march on Washington, Kennedy called a private meeting to urge black leaders not to hold the march. To placate the president, Dr. Martin Luther King Jr. and the other black leaders agreed to censor speeches calling for civil unrest and congressional office protests. But Kennedy was still worried. He feared that the march could create a political backlash with white Americans. During the meeting, Kennedy said, "The Vice-President and I know what it will mean if we fail [to pass the Civil Rights Act]. I have just seen a new poll—national approval of the administration has fallen from 60 to 47 per cent. We're in this up to our neck."[7] The president also indicated that he thought it was "a terrible mistake" that the march had been announced before the civil rights bill had made its way to committee.[8]

Kennedy and Johnson's concerns over a potential fault line in the Democratic Party proved prescient. But following Kennedy's assassination, President Lyndon Johnson decided to move forward with the bill. Like the Democratic Party, Johnson had been a relative latecomer to the cause of civil rights. According to LBJ biographer Robert Caro, before 1957 Johnson "had never supported civil rights legislation—any civil rights legislation. In Senate and House alike, his record was an unbroken one of votes against every civil rights bill that had ever come to a vote: against voting rights bills; against bills that would have struck at job discrimination and at segregation in other areas of American life; even against bills that would have protected blacks from lynching."[9]

Johnson's private behavior toward African Americans had been equally hateful. Robert Parker, Johnson's longtime black employee and limousine chauffeur, states in his autobiography that Johnson "called me 'boy,' 'ni——r,' or 'chief,' never by my name. . . . Whenever I was late, no matter what the reason, Johnson called me a lazy, good-for-nothing ni——r. . . . Although I was grateful to him for getting me a job . . . I was afraid of him because of the pain and humiliation he could inflict at a moment's notice."[10]

Still, Johnson had made the decision to support the bill Kennedy had initiated. Passing the legislation should have been easy for Democrats. As Senate minority leader Dirksen noted:

> First, let me point out that in this Senate are 67 members bearing the Democrat label. It takes only a majority to enact the Administration bill, namely 51. It takes 67 to impose cloture if cloture is needed. I say to the President, that his Party has enough members to do both jobs. If as he has said to me, the job cannot be done without Republicans, perhaps he should turn the reins of government over to Republicans. With such a top-heavy majority, we should not find it necessary to turn to his Party for results.[11]

Johnson's obstacle in passing the Civil Rights Act of 1964 came not from Republicans, but from Democrats. As the president's own voting record revealed, like Senator Byrd, Democrats had long opposed the party of Lincoln's efforts to grant African Americans equal rights. In the House, of the 420 voting members, the bill had passed by a 290 to 130 vote. House Republicans supported the bill by a 138 to 34 margin. Democrats, however, had been more divided, voting 152 for and 96 against passing the civil rights law. When the bill reached the Senate, Senator Byrd stood ready to kill it. Six Republicans, including Barry Goldwater, had objected to the bill on the philosophical grounds of federal overreach. But it had been the twenty-two Democrats, including Al Gore Sr., who had linked arms with the segregationist leader Byrd to ensure the bill's defeat through a Senate filibuster.

The chances of stopping Byrd's filibuster seemed bleak—impossible even. Never in the history of the U.S. Senate had members mustered enough votes to kill a filibuster on a civil rights bill. Moreover, since 1927 only once had the Senate agreed to cloture on any measure.[12] For this reason, *cloture* remains a term with which few Americans are familiar. The seldom used standing Senate rule was created during a filibuster against the 1917 armed ship bill. The maneuver was designed to prevent possible obstructionist minorities in the Senate from grinding widely supported legislation to a halt. At the time of Byrd's filibuster of the Civil Rights Act of 1964, a cloture vote required sixty-seven votes (two-thirds of the Senate) to pass. As President Johnson and Democratic Senate majority leader Mike Mansfield both understood, the fact that the administration couldn't enforce party obeisance meant only one thing according Mansfield: "The key is Dirksen."[13]

That Everett Dirksen would become one of the Republican Party's brightest stars seemed predestined. His parents, Johann and Antje, both German immigrants, had named their sons after famous GOP figures: Everett's middle name was McKinley; his twin brother was named after Republican Speaker of the House Thomas Reed; and his oldest brother was Benjamin Harrison Dirksen. "I come of immigrant German stock," said Dirksen, "My mother stood on Ellis Island as a child of 17, with a tag around her neck directing that she be sent to Pekin, Illinois."[14] And so it was that Everett Dirksen, "the pride of Pekin," would launch his political career in the land of Lincoln.

Dirksen attended the University of Minnesota before enlisting in the army, where he was commissioned overseas as a second lieutenant. After his return to Pekin, he participated in the Pekin centennial play *A Thousand Years Ago*. There, he met Louella Carver, whom he married in 1927. Following an initial failed run for a U.S. House seat, in 1932 Dirksen was elected to his first of eight consecutive terms. By 1950, he made the leap to the U.S. Senate and was later elected as Senate minority leader, a position he held until his death in 1969.

Over the span of his nearly four decades of public service, Dirksen gained a reputation as "the Senate's most practiced and professional orator."[15] His deep and deliberative vocal quality was sometimes compared to the voice of Mr. Ed. His tussled, wavy hair, thick black frame glasses, and wrinkle-prone attire hardly projected an image of power and command. But many of Dirksen's associates believed his disheveled outward appearance had all been part of a studied ploy to disarm and lower expectations. Indeed, the leader's communicative prowess revealed a prepared and strategic thinker. And it was these skills, combined with his strong knowledge of Senate rules, that assisted Dirksen in halting a five-month-long filibuster—the longest in the history of the U.S. Senate. Ironically, the Illinois Republican who carried the pro-equality mantle of Lincoln, would come to the aid of a Democratic president, Lyndon Johnson.[16] But without Dirksen, the passage of the Civil Rights Act of 1964 might never have been possible.

Johnson was acutely aware of how badly he needed Dirksen to defeat his own party's filibuster. Besides his own legendary "personal touch" (some would call it "arm twisting"), President Johnson enlisted the help of others in reaching out to Dirksen to get him to somehow deliver two-thirds of the thirty-three Republican senators to support the civil rights law.

"Now you know this bill can't pass unless you get Ev Dirksen," Johnson told Hubert Humphrey. "You and I are going to get him. You make up your mind now that you've got to spend time with Ev Dirksen. You've got to let him have a piece of the action. He's got to look good all the time," the president said. And so, for example, when Humphrey appeared on NBC's *Meet the Press*, Humphrey laid on the praise extra thick: "He [Dirksen] is a man who thinks of his country before he thinks of his party. He is one who understands the legislative process intimately and fully, and I sincerely believe that when Senator Dirksen has to face that moment of decision where his influence and where his leadership will be required in order to give us the votes that are necessary to pass the bill, he will not be found wanting." Following the interview, President Johnson called Humphrey: "Boy, that was right. You're doing just right now. You just keep at that. Don't you let those bomb throwers, now, talk you out of seeing Dirksen. You get in there to see Dirksen! You drink with Dirksen! You talk to Dirksen! You listen to Dirksen!"[17]

For his own part, Johnson, too, had resorted to lobbying Dirksen by attempting to appeal to the Illinois senator's legacy and place in history. According to historian Michael Beschloss, in the spring of 1964 Johnson called Dirksen and in effect said, "Ev, I know you've got some doubts, but look at it this way, if this bill passes it's going to change the country and make history, and if all that happens everyone will give credit to you. And if it happens, a hundred years from now the school children of America will know exactly two names, Abraham Lincoln and Everett Dirksen."[18] While the parallel reference to Illinois's most famous politician, Lincoln, might have pleased Dirksen, the hyperbolic promise was hardly what motivated the Republican minority leader to take on the Herculean task of delivering the necessary GOP votes.

When Republicans expressed serious concerns about the bill's vague language, Dirksen took offense when some Democrats, newspapers, and civil rights groups began attacking him and the Republican Party as not having lived up to its civil rights heritage. After hearing one such attack, Dirksen wrote in a private notebook:

Who may I ask freed the slaves? Who may I ask set in motion the Emancipation Proclamation? Who may I ask initiated the 13th, 14th, and 15th Amendments to the Constitution to provide safeguards for their freedom and equality? Who initiated the first meaningful and substantial Civil Rights legislation in 80 years if it was not done by President Eisenhower? Who gave impetus to the school desegregation cases if it was not a Republican Attorney General?...Our record on Civil Rights will stand up beside your record at anytime.[19]

Dirksen was incensed. The Democratic Party and many in the black civil rights movement were playing a Machiavellian shell game of history. All along, the GOP had been the party who freed the slaves and fought alongside African Americans to earn the rights and privileges they were due. But now, in an act of extreme political expediency, some Democrats and black organizations such as the National Association for the Advancement of Colored People (NAACP) were harshly attacking Dirksen and the other Senate Republicans. It was the Democrats whose most distinguished and high-ranking party leader was working to deny blacks full entry into American life. But that mattered little. Indeed, despite the fact that he seldom received support from Chicago's black voters, Dirksen believed that the issue of equality transcended partisan politics. Civil rights was a moral imperative.

Dirksen wasn't the only Republican LBJ needed to win passage of the bill. With over one-third of senate Democrats jockeying to defeat the measure, Dirksen had to convince the majority of Senate Republicans to join him in supporting the bill. This was difficult for two reasons. First, Republicans fully understood that they would get little credit among black voters for saving the bill from defeat. History assigns undue credit and blame to presidents, not members of Congress; Americans remember the names of presidents before they do representatives and senators. And second, because of the bill's ceding of enforcement to the federal government, Dirksen knew that conservatives would be nervous about federal encroachment on the rights of states to enforce laws.

As for his own personal ideology, Dirksen described himself as a sort of pragmatic conservative: "I consider myself a conservative, probably not as conservative as some, not as moderately liberal or liberally moderate as others. You see after all, a party leader has a job. There are viewpoints over here and viewpoints over there, but I think your first responsibility is to develop a degree of unity and cohesion in your party."[20]

And that's what Dirksen did. He began rounding up members and asking them what modifications had to be made in the bill's language before they could support the measure. Yet, even as Dirksen led the way on offering amendments to the bill's specific language, and even with Humphrey encouraging Democrats and blacks to hold their fire and not antagonize the minority leader as he labored to cobble together a coalition, Democratic attacks against Dirksen and other Republicans continued. Undeterred, Dirksen soldiered on. "I have a fixed polestar to which I am pointed," Dirksen said. "And this is it: first to get a bill, second to get an acceptable bill, third to get a workable bill, and finally to get an equitable bill."[21]

The night before the final vote, the sixty-eight-year-old Dirksen stayed up late into the night typing a speech on twelve sheets of Senate stationery. Motivating and inspiring his words was the memory of his young, immigrant mother standing on a windswept Ellis Island. "Our family had opportunities in Illinois, and the essence of what we're trying to do in the civil rights bill is to see that others have opportunities in this country," Dirksen later explained.[22]

On the seventy-fifth day of debate, June 10, 1964, the Senate had finally arrived at the anxiously anticipated roll call vote on cloture. Historian John G. Stewart recounts that "[a]n air of drama and expectancy suffused the Senate chamber to a degree seldom experienced by even the most senior members. The public galleries had been filled for hours. Outside on the Capitol lawn, a TV reporter stood ready to relay to the nation a vote-by-vote capitulation of the roll call." Roger Mudd, the CBS-TV newsman, was prepared to receive a verbal report of each vote via telephone from the press gallery. He then planned to tally the votes on a cloture scoreboard CBS had set up on the lawn. Senatorial staff assistants, who were blocked from entering the Senate floor during the vote and who had been unable to squeeze into the jammed public galleries, were forced to watch Mudd's television report from Senate offices.[23]

Fifteen minutes before the historic vote, Senator Dirksen was the last senator to deliver a floor speech before the voting began. Playing the role of historian, Dirksen began his speech with a historical recitation of the long and "torturous road" the bill had taken to arrive at the present decisive moment:

> *Mr. President, it is a year ago this month that the late President Kennedy sent his civil rights bill and message to the Congress. For two years, we had been chiding him about failure to act in this field. At long last, and after many conferences, it became a reality.*

Dirksen cataloged the laundry list of House and Senate committees and subcommittees and motions to consider the bill. Then, in a series of terse sentences, the minority leader popped off the results of Byrd's filibuster:

> *Sharp opinions have developed. Incredible allegations have been made. Extreme views have been asserted. The mail volume has been heavy. The bill has provoked many long-distance telephone calls, many of them late at night or in the small hours of the morning. There has been unrestrained criticism about motives.*

From there, the minority leader established his own ethos on the issue of civil rights. In a not-so-veiled shot across the Democratic bow, and at Johnson in particular, Dirksen set the record straight:

> *I am no Johnnie-come-lately in this field. Thirty years ago, in the House of Representatives, I voted on anti-poll tax and anti-lynching measures. Since then, I have sponsored or co-sponsored scores of bills dealing with civil rights.*

Dirksen recognized that only once in the last thirty-five years had cloture been voted. But, he added, "There are many reasons why cloture should be invoked and a good civil rights measure enacted." The body of his speech then advanced four reasons senators should vote for cloture on the Civil Rights Act of 1964:

> *First. It is said that on the night he died, Victor Hugo wrote in his diary, substantially this sentiment:* Stronger than all the armies is an idea whose time has come. *The time has come for equality of opportunity in sharing in government, in education, and in employment. It will not be stayed or denied. It is here. The problem began when the Constitution makers permitted the importation of persons to continue for another twenty years. The problem was to generate the fury of civil strife seventy-five years later. Out of it was to come the Thirteenth Amendment ending servitude, the Fourteenth Amendment to provide equal protection of the laws and dual citizenship, the Fifteenth Amendment to prohibit government from abridging the right to vote. . . . To enact the pending measure by invoking cloture is imperative.*

The quotation from Victor Hugo, the famous French Romantic writer of the nineteenth century, established a running thesis—"an idea whose time has come"—that Dirksen returned to several times throughout his speech. And just as he had recorded previously in his private notebook, Dirksen reminded Americans of the historic advances Republicans won for black advancement and equality:

> *Second. . . . Nothing is eternal except change. . . . America has changed. The population then [1875] was 45 million. Today it is 190 million. In the Pledge of Allegiance to the Flag we intone, "One nation, under God." And so it is. It is an integrated nation. Air, rail, and highway transportation make it so. A common language makes it so. The mobility provided by 80*

million autos makes it so. The accommodations laws in thirty-four states and the District of Columbia makes it so. The fair employment practice laws in thirty states make it so. Yes, our land has changed since the Supreme Court decision of 1883.

As Lincoln once observed: "The occasion is piled high with difficulty and we must rise with the occasion. As our case is new, so we must think anew and act anew. We must first disenthrall ourselves and then we shall save the Union." To my friends from the South, I would refresh you on the words of a great Georgian named Henry W. Grady. . . . His words were dramatic and explosive. He began his toast by saying: There was a South of slavery and secession—that South is dead. There is a South of union and freedom—that South thank God is living, breathing, growing every hour.

America grows. America changes. And on the civil rights issue we must rise with the occasion. That calls for cloture and for the enactment of a civil rights bill.

By quoting passages from well-known leaders, Dirksen established a precedent for change and the advancement of civil rights. Like Lincoln, Dirksen considered himself a conservative; he believed in conserving the spirit of freedom and equality imparted by God at the time of an individual's creation. Thus, conserving the God-ordained rights of man, not the man-made institution of slavery, represented the true path of Republican conservatism. For southern Democrats, Dirksen's reference to Henry W. Grady offered them a principled historical path to follow that could lead the Democratic Party to finally reject the institutions of oppression that their party had built and long supported.

Third. There is another reason—our covenant with the people. . . . Go back and reexamine our pledges to the country as we sought the suffrage of the people and for a grant of authority to manage and direct their affairs. Were these pledges so much campaign stuff or did we mean it? Were these promises on civil rights but idle words for vote-getting purposes or were they a covenant meant to be kept? If all this was mere pretense, let us confess the sin of hypocrisy now and vow not to delude the people again. To you, my Republican colleagues, let me refresh you on the words of a great American. His name is Herbert Hoover. In his day he was reviled and maligned. He was castigated and calumniated. But today his views and his judgment stand vindicated at the bar of history: "The Whig party temporized, compromised upon the issue of the freedom for the Negro. That party disappeared. It deserved to disappear. Shall the Republican party receive or deserve any better fate if it compromises upon the issue of freedom for all men?"

To those who have charged me with doing a disservice to my party because of my interest in the enactment of a good civil rights bill—and there have been a good many who have made that charge—I can only say that our party found its faith in the Declaration of Independence. . . . That has been the living faith of our party. Do we forsake this article of faith, now that equality's time has come or do we stand up for it and insure the survival of our party and its ultimate victory. There is no substitute for a basic and righteous idea. We have a duty—a firm duty— to use the instruments at hand—namely, the cloture rule—to bring about the enactment of a good civil rights bill.

By framing the bill as a religious question over a "righteous idea," Dirksen further moralized the bill. Inaction or defeat of the bill, he argued, was tantamount to breaking a "covenant" and would require senators to "confess the sin of hypocrisy."

In addition, Dirksen guarded himself from the sharp criticisms he had received from some Republicans who worried that handing a Democratic president a major victory on the civil rights bill would allow Democrats to claim credit for a bill that was Republican to its core. Given Johnson's appalling civil rights voting record, some Republicans viewed LBJ's support as little more than a public relations gambit designed to cover over his and the Democratic Party's history of oppressing blacks. Critiques of Johnson's Machiavellian public relations tactics on issues of race were not without justification. As the *New York Times* recounted, on the issue of why he had appointed Thurgood Marshall to the Supreme Court, President Johnson had once told an aide: "Son, when I appoint a ni——r to the court, I want everyone to know he's a ni——r."[24]

> *Fourth. There is another reason why we dare not temporize with the issue which is before us. It is essentially moral in character. It must be resolved. It will not go away. Its time has come.*

This refrain—"Its time has come"—became the repeating phrase used to punctuate the next five passages. This rhetorical device, known as an antistrophe, involves the repetition of a phrase at the end of sentences or passages in succession. With the historic roll call vote just minutes away, Dirksen's use of parallel repetition pounded home the urgency of the moment. In the intervening passages between the repeating phrase, Dirksen walked his audience through a series of famous legislative battles that had seemed outrageous and revolutionary at the time of their debating, but that had later proven to be key turning points in ensuring essential rights for Americans.

The minority leader's speech then turned homeward to his state's most famous resident, Abraham Lincoln, to point out a coincidence of history. As it happened, June 10, 1964, marked the one-hundredth anniversary of the Republican nomination of Lincoln for a second term as president. Dirksen then cited a passage from the Gettysburg Address to further illustrate to his Republican colleagues that voting to support the Civil Rights Act of 1964, while not likely to yield electoral dividends with black voters, was to act in accord with the party's founding purpose: to promote an end to slavery. Dirksen argued that Republican senators were once again being called to do the heavy lifting of history, just as the GOP had done a century ago. "It is to take us further down that road that a bill is pending before us," Dirksen said. "We have a duty to get that job done. I trust we shall not fail in that duty."

Dirksen presented GOP solidarity on the civil rights vote as a way of remaining true to Republicanism's first principles. He equated support for the legislation with keeping faith with the Republican Party's founding. He then concluded with a final call to action directed toward all senators:

> There is no substitute for a basic ideal. We have a firm duty to use the instrument at hand; namely, the cloture rule, to bring about the enactment of a good civil rights bill. I appeal to all senators. We are confronted with a moral issue. Today let us not be found wanting in whatever it takes by way of moral and spiritual substance to face up to the issue and to vote cloture.

Immediately following Senator Dirksen's speech, the Senate clerk proceeded to call the roll. The final tally: 71 to 29, a full four votes more than were needed to end Senator Byrd's filibuster. Nine days later, the Senate passed the Civil Rights Act of 1964, a bill that forever changed the lives of African Americans.

Following Dirksen's speech and the passage of the bill, Democratic majority leader Mansfield said, "This is his [Dirksen's] finest hour. The Senate, the whole country is in debt to the Senator from Illinois." In a rare moment of gratitude and apology, two days after Senator Dirksen's historic speech, Roy Wilkins of the NAACP wrote Dirksen a contrite letter:

> Let me be the first to admit that I was in error in estimating your preliminary announcements and moves. . . . The resounding vote of 71–29 June 10 to shut off debate tended mightily to reinforce your judgment and to vindicate your procedure. It is significant that 27 of the 33 Republican Senators voted for cloture, the first time it has ever been imposed on a civil rights bill debate. The National Association for the Advancement of Colored People sends its thanks to you for your vote for cloture and for your final speech before the vote. . . . As you well noted, the time of an idea

has come. . . . Your leadership of the Republican Party in the Senate at this turning point will become a significant part of the history of this century.[25]

Time magazine agreed. It ran a picture of Dirksen on its cover the following week. In that issue, *Time* wrote that Dirksen's speech delivered just fifteen minutes before the vote "more than anyone else's had made a favorable cloture vote likely."[26]

Dirksen's name is unknown to most Americans today. But as a *Chicago Daily News* editorial conceded, without his leadership the Civil Rights Act of 1964 would have never been passed: "It wasn't long ago that Dirksen was the target of abuse from the more vocal liberals who said he was against civil rights. They were wrong . . . without him the civil rights bill would have [had] no chance."[27]

6

Barry Goldwater

"You Know He's Right"

"Extremism in the Defense of Liberty Is No Vice"

JULY 16, 1964

REPUBLICAN NATIONAL CONVENTION, THE COW PALACE,
SAN FRANCISCO, CALIFORNIA

I have little interest in streamlining government or making
it more efficient, for I mean to reduce its size. . . . My aim
is not to pass laws, but to repeal them.

—Barry Goldwater, *The Conscience of a Conservative*

Barry Goldwater was the most consequential presidential loser in American history. Without a Goldwater candidacy, many agree, Ronald Reagan might never have become president.[1] Moreover, Goldwater may have been the only presidential candidate who didn't want to be president, nor believed he could be. To be sure, "Mr. Conservative," as he was popularly known, was an original. At the dawn of the televised presidency, Goldwater's blunt, prickly, straight-talking style defied the heavily scripted, politically correct sound-bite culture of the media. "This is going to be a campaign of principles, not personalities," Goldwater once growled to a young staffer during his 1964 presidential run. "I don't want that kind of Madison Avenue stuff, and if you try it, I will kick your ass out of the office."[2] But beyond stylistics, Goldwater's fierce brand of individualism and uncompromising passion for freedom and liberty gave birth to the conservative movement that defines the modern Republican Party.

Standing six feet tall, with steel blue eyes, bronze skin, and a silver shock of hair, the square-jawed former World War II pilot's physical appearance reflected the rugged individualism that typified the state he loved so much: Arizona. During his eulogy of Barry Goldwater, Senator John McCain, a political heir of Goldwater's maverick style, recounted how Goldwater would sometimes get emotional when discussing his deep affection for the state of Arizona. "Arizona is 113,400 square miles of heaven that God cut out," Goldwater said as he fought back tears. "I love it so much."[3] The only thing greater than Goldwater's passion for Arizona, it seemed, was the conservative movement's passion for Barry Goldwater.

Barry Goldwater's biographer, Lee Edwards, put it this way: "While it is commonly said that Goldwater created the modern conservative movement, it might be more accurate to say that the movement created itself through the Goldwater campaign. It became a substantial political force for the first time, and it learned from Goldwater's heroic example that not to shrink from battle is itself a victory."[4]

That's not to suggest that conservative Republicans never had their problems with Goldwater. Particularly during his later years, Goldwater's outspoken, brash style made some Republicans wonder whether he had betrayed the conservative movement he helped create. The Arizonan's cantankerous statements sometimes read more like a Democratic Party fund-raising letter than the words of a conservative icon. For example, following Sandra Day O'Connor's nomination to the U.S. Supreme Court in 1981, Moral Majority founder Jerry Falwell told reporters that "every good Christian should be concerned." Replied Goldwater: "Every good Christian should line up and kick Jerry Falwell's ass."[5] About Richard M. Nixon he once said, "As far as I'm concerned, Nixon can go to China and stay there." On Newt Gingrich: he "talks too much." Goldwater's pro-choice position on abortion and outspoken support for gay rights also placed him at odds with many in the Republican Party. Yet to the end, Goldwater maintained that his views represented the true spirit of conservatism, limited government, and personal freedom and liberty.[6]

But it had been the other side of Goldwater's rhetorical blade that had so captured conservative hearts and minds. His salty and stirring conservative proclamations became the clarion call that spawned a new generation of conservative Republicans. About PBS commentator Bill Moyers, who had also been an aide to Lyndon Johnson, Goldwater said, "Every time I see him, I get sick to my stomach and want to throw up." And Jane Fonda, Goldwater once explained, was nothing but a "political whore." But more than his penchant for hurling verbal daggers, it had been the serious and striking words of his best-selling book *The Conscience of a Conservative* that had electrified and galvanized the American conservative movement. Promising "a choice, not an echo," the book's first printing of 10,000 copies proved insufficient to meet reader demand; the book sold over 3.5 million copies, became a best seller at college bookstores, and made Goldwater the most demanded speaker on college campuses. As Richard Brookhiser wrote, "The conservative movement, when it was first moving, was to a great extent a youth crusade. . . . Goldwater's hold on the young was rhetorical and intellectual."[7]

Published in 1960, *The Conscience of a Conservative* laid out a new and revolutionary conservative vision that gave Goldwater a presidential platform on which to run:

> I have little interest in streamlining government or making it more efficient, for I mean to reduce its size. I do not undertake to promote welfare, for I propose to extend freedom. My aim is not to pass laws, but to repeal them. It is not to inaugurate new programs, but to cancel old ones that do violence to the Constitution, or that have failed in their purpose, or that impose on the people an unwarranted financial burden. I will not attempt to discover whether legislation is "needed" before I have first determined whether it is constitutionally permissible. And if I should later be attacked for neglecting my constituents interests, I shall reply that I was informed their main interest is liberty and that in that cause, I am doing the very best I can.[8]

In October 1961, twenty well-connected, conservative Republicans, who had taken to calling themselves the "hard core," gathered in

Chicago to discuss how they could bottle the passion and excitement Goldwater's message had created among Republicans and translate it into a majority of delegates at the next national convention. They decided that only Goldwater could carry the conservative banner. But Goldwater had no interest in becoming president of the United States. He loved the Senate, didn't think he was smart enough to be president (he had flunked out of high school his freshman year), and thought that President John F. Kennedy, and later President Johnson, would crush him.[9]

By mid-February 1963, the group met for the last time in Chicago. After endless hours trying to figure out how best to persuade Goldwater to run for president, an exasperated Robert Hughes of Indiana finally growled, "There's only one thing we *can* do. Let's draft the son of a bitch."[10] F. Clifton White, whom Lee Edwards once described as "a tall, bow-tied professional politician from New York who taught politics at Cornell and then worked in the presidential campaigns of Dewey, Eisenhower, and Nixon," traveled the country on behalf of the Draft Goldwater movement. Following President Kennedy's assassination, however, Goldwater sensed that his presidential run would be hopeless. So the Arizona senator made his intentions clear: "Pass the word," he told his head organizer and old friend, Denison Kitchel, Goldwater will not run. But when the millions of conservatives to whom Goldwater was now an icon responded, Kitchel told the senator he didn't think he had much of a choice. "Barry," Kitchel told him, "I don't think you can back down." Frustrated, Goldwater huffed, "All right, damn it. I'll do it."[11]

Even as Goldwater was securing the Republican nomination, Everett Dirksen had been busy steering the Civil Rights Act of 1964 to safe passage. Goldwater had been one of only six Republicans whom Dirksen could not convince to support the landmark legislation. As even Dr. Martin Luther King Jr. conceded, Goldwater was not a racist. The Arizona senator's record on issues of equality were well known. Goldwater had supported both the 1957 and 1960 civil rights acts.

As chief of staff for the Arizona Air National Guard, Goldwater had been two years ahead of President Harry Truman when the Arizonan began pushing for desegregation of the guard. In addition, Goldwater had served and hired African Americans at his family's Goldwater department store, and had himself been a generous contributor to the Arizona chapter of the NAACP and to the Phoenix division of the Urban League.[12]

Still, using the opinions of his legal advisers, such as William Rehnquist and Robert Bork, Goldwater decided to oppose the Civil Rights Act of 1964 because he believed it violated states' rights and property rights. As Goldwater explained to an audience during one rally, "You cannot pass a law that will make me like you—or you like me. That is something that can only happen in our hearts." Understanding the inherent injustice in reverse discrimination policies, such as affirmative action, the Arizonan then warned prophetically, "It reintroduces through the back door the very principle of allocation by race that makes compulsory segregation morally wrong and offensive to freedom. Our aim as I understand it, is neither to establish a segregated society nor to establish an integrated society. It is to preserve a free society."[13]

Before voting against the Civil Rights Act of 1964, Senator Goldwater said, "I am unalterably opposed to discrimination of any sort." Still, he could not in good conscience support provisions that would "fly in the face of the Constitution, and which would require for their effective execution the creation of a police state."[14] Despite his principled, philosophical reasons for doing so, Goldwater's vote was interpreted as insensitive to African Americans and a rejection of the Lincolnian ideals of the Republican Party. "Barry, this is a dreadful mistake," liberal Republican senator Jacob Javits warned him.[15] But Goldwater was nothing if not unbending; his decision had been made. His vote unintentionally sent a harsh signal to young African American voters. When, for example, a young Colin Powell received word that Goldwater had been one of only a handful of Republicans to vote against the bill, Powell says he put an "All the Way with LBJ" bumper sticker on the back of his Volkswagen.[16]

The electoral consequences of Goldwater's highly publicized vote against the Civil Rights Act of 1964 proved seismic and long lasting for the Republican Party. According to the Joint Center for Political and Economic Studies, in 1960, 32 percent of African American voters supported the Republican Party. When Goldwater ran in 1964, African American support for the GOP plunged to an all-time low of only 6 percent.[17]

These results had been influenced by Dr. King's urging of black Americans to vote for Johnson. "While not himself a racist, Mr. Goldwater articulated a philosophy which gave aid and comfort to the racist," King wrote. "His candidacy and philosophy would serve as an umbrella under which extremists of all stripes would stand. In the light of these facts and because of my love for America, I had no alternative but to urge every Negro and white person of goodwill to vote against Mr. Goldwater and to withdraw support from any Republican candidate that did not publicly disassociate himself from Senator Goldwater and his philosophy."[18] And with that, like the infamous "Daisy" television advertisement that depicted a megaton bomb exploding into a mushroom cloud, the historic union between the Republican Party and African Americans that had eroded since the 1930s was officially obliterated.

Not fully understanding the power of political symbolism and the new emerging rules of image politics in a television age, Goldwater had been mortified that his vote against the bill morphed into a magnet for antiblack sentiment. Behind-the-scenes reporter Glenn Garvin recalls:

> Goldwater was privately appalled to discover that his opposition to the Civil Rights Act rallied to his side not only libertarians but racists who detested and feared not state power but black people. He was horrified when Alabama's racist Governor George Wallace offered to switch parties and run as his vice president. Goldwater eventually became so paranoid about the influx of racists to his campaign that he worried that a summer riot in Harlem had been secretly instigated by his supporters in hopes of generating a white backlash vote.[19]

It was against this fiery backdrop that Goldwater delivered what conservative movement historian Lee Edwards dubbed "the most quoted and controversial acceptance speech in the history of national conventions."[20] Besides being portrayed as an extremist on civil rights, Goldwater's pull-no-punches rhetoric on Communism, welfare, Social Security, and crime gave Johnson and the Democratic Party all the ammunition they needed to attack Goldwater's brand of conservatism as a radical far-Right nightmare that Americans should reject. But it would be Goldwater's words, spoken on July 16, 1964, at the Cow Palace in San Francisco, California, that would give the Arizonan his largest audience ever, and with it twenty-seven million supporters who would later become the foot soldiers of future conservative causes and the Reagan Revolution.

William F. Buckley's brother-in-law, Brent Bozell, ghostwrote Goldwater's *Conscience of a Conservative*, but it was Harry Jaffe, a former student of Leo Strauss, the philosophical "godfather" of neoconservatism, who penned Goldwater's 1964 Republican National Convention acceptance speech. Writing speeches for Goldwater was not without its risks. Following his boss's smashing presidential defeat, Karl Hess, Goldwater's chief speechwriter, had been so maligned for his role in the Republican routing that after he was denied numerous writing positions, he eventually enrolled in a night school welding course and took a job working the night shift in a machine shop. [21] While Jaffe, a professor of political philosophy at Claremont-McKenna College, fared better professionally, but even he confessed that for years after writing the Goldwater speech he could not convince editors to publish his articles or commentary.[22]

To politically inoculate the nominee from backlash over his decision not to support the Civil Rights Act of 1964, Goldwater's campaign tapped Senator Dirksen to nominate Goldwater for president at the Republican National Convention. In an attempt to reframe Goldwater's vote against the bill, Dirksen described the presidential nominee's vote on the bill as an example of "moral courage not excelled anywhere in any parliamentary body of which I have any knowledge. . . . Delegates to this convention," Dirksen boomed, "the tide is turning! . . . Let's give 190 million Americans the choice they have been waiting for!"[23] The next night, Goldwater painted the air with the words of his conservative vision. As he did, he ushered in a young breed of ironclad conservatives. After extending his thanks and formally accepting the Republican Party nomination, Goldwater carved out the major themes of his address:

> In this world no person, no Party can guarantee anything, but what we can do and what we shall do is to deserve victory, and victory will be ours.
>
> The good Lord raised this mighty Republic to be a home for the brave and to flourish as the land of the free—not to stagnate in the swampland of collectivism, not to cringe before the bullying of communism.
>
> Now, my fellow Americans, the tide has been running against freedom. Our people have followed false prophets. We must, and we shall, return to proven ways—not because they are old, but because they are true. We must, and we shall, set the tides running again in the cause of freedom.

The first line was politically and philosophically loaded. Politically, it was meant to underscore Goldwater's plainspoken, honest style. While journalists often characterized Goldwater as an unpolished orator with a flat and fumbling speaking style, many conceded these qualities made the Arizona senator appear convincing, sincere, effective, believable, and ingratiating.[24] But this sentence also reflects the philosophical underpinnings of American conservatism, which hold that while citizens should be guaranteed equal opportunities, citizens must never be guaranteed equal outcomes. The difference between these two visions represents the difference between democracy/capitalism and socialism/Communism, or, in slightly softer terms, individualism versus collectivism.[25]

The Republican candidate's next sentence is also striking. It boldly declares a belief in American exceptionalism—the notion that the United States is a God-blessed nation whose history and founding bear the fingerprints of Providence. The second half of the sentence further illustrates Goldwater's thematic bifurcation between self-determinism and individualism (the conservative vision) versus government controls and prescribed outcomes (the liberal versus Communist vision). To bring it all home, Goldwater's final line casts his political opponents as "false prophets." Next, Goldwater declared that Americans must become "freedom's missionaries in a doubting world":

> *Now, failures cement the wall of shame in Berlin. Failures blot the sands of shame at the Bay of Pigs. Failures mark the slow death of freedom in Laos. Failures infest the jungles of Vietnam. And failures haunt the houses of our once great alliances and undermine the greatest bulwark ever erected by free nations— the NATO community. Failures proclaim lost leadership, obscure purpose, weakening will, and the risk of inciting our sworn enemies to new aggressions and to new excesses. . . . We are plodding along at a pace set by centralized planning, red tape, rules without responsibility, and regimentation without recourse.*
>
> *Rather than useful jobs in our country, our people have been offered bureaucratic "make work"; rather than moral leadership, they have been given bread and circuses. They have been given spectacles, and, yes, they've even been given scandals.*
>
> *Tonight, there is violence in our streets, corruption in our highest offices, aimlessness amongst our youth, anxiety among our elders, and there's a virtual despair among the many who look beyond material success for the inner meaning of their lives.*

Following the structure of the classic jeremiad—a speech structure that begins by citing the myriad woes of the land only to then unfold a path for achieving a bright and prosperous future—Goldwater first catalogs a list of U.S. foreign policy failures under Democratic leadership before bringing those distant failures closer home to America's shores. The GOP candidate even goes further by showing how the values embedded in public policy can translate into the inner life of each citizen:

> *Republicans see all this as more, much more, than the result of mere political differences or mere political mistakes. We see this as the result of a fundamentally and absolutely wrong view of man, his nature, and his destiny. Those who seek to live your lives for you, to take your liberties in return for relieving you of yours, those who elevate the state and downgrade the citizen must see ultimately a world in which earthly power can be substituted for Divine Will, and this Nation was founded upon the rejection of that notion and upon the acceptance of God as the author of freedom. . . .*
>
> *It is the cause of Republicanism to ensure that power remains in the hands of the people. . . . It is further the cause of Republicanism to restore a clear understanding of the tyranny of man over man in the world at large. It is our cause to dispel the foggy thinking which avoids hard decisions in the delusion that a world of conflict will somehow mysteriously resolve itself into a world of harmony, if we just don't rock the boat or irritate the forces of aggression—and this is hogwash. It is further the cause of Republicanism to remind ourselves, and the world, that only the strong can remain free, that only the strong can keep the peace.*

With a healthy infusion of Jaffe-inspired Straussian philosophy, Goldwater delivered a brand of philosophical rhetoric seldom heard in political speeches today. Still, the speech drove straight to the core distinction between Republicans (individualists) and Democrats (collectivists). And that distinction involved a vision of the world that sees its inhabitants as innately flawed, self-interested, and therefore dependent on God for direction and salvation. By contrast, collectivism asserts a worldview in which human nature is malleable and therefore able to be perfected through man-made institutions, such as governmental agencies and programs, while still on earth. Again, this was heady discourse for a presidential campaign speech. But the deep ideological root structure of Goldwater's speech is what gave it its richness and strength. This was especially true for conservatives who, before Goldwater, had never had a presidential spokesman.

In addition, Goldwater put forward a simple if profound formulation for foreign policy and the fighting of wars: fight to win; strength equals peace. Ronald Reagan would later use this foreign policy equation to fashion his mantra "Peace through Strength." By attacking Democratic pacifism as a form of wistful idealism, Goldwater sounded the conservative note of being prepared to use aggressive action to achieve peaceful ends. These themes seem well established to contemporary readers, but at the time, these principles struck many Americans as entirely new, thought provoking, and innovative. Those who found Goldwater's pronouncements in this light became newly minted conservatives.

> *My fellow Republicans, we do no man a service by hiding freedom's light under a bushel of mistaken humility.*
>
> *I seek an America proud of its past, proud of its ways, proud of its dreams, and determined actively to proclaim them. But our example to the world must, like charity, begin at home. . . .*
>
> *We must assure a society here which, while never abandoning the needy or forsaking the helpless, nurtures incentives and opportunities for the creative and the productive. We must know the whole good is the product of many single contributions.*

The first line of this passage is yet another biblical allusion, this time from Matthew 5:15: "Neither do men light a lamp, and put it under the bushel, but on the stand; and it shineth unto all that are in the house." This artful use of scriptural reference underscores the need to proclaim and declare one's beliefs with pride and confidence. Today this remains a central feature of Republican rhetoric. The shrinking, self-loathing moral relativism endemic to so much of liberal rhetoric often elides the celebratory "tone poems" to freedom and individualism often associated with Republican oratory. Liberal Democrats characterize these rhetorical flourishes as "breathless patriotism" or garish "flag waving." But to the conservative, especially the Evangelical Christian—whose very name means "to evangelize" (share, proclaim)—patriotic proclamations of freedom aren't just tolerated, they're welcomed.

Despite the abundance of Christian allusions, Goldwater's later criticism of the so-called Religious Right led some to suggest that he was the closest thing to a Libertarian presidential candidate the United States has ever known, preferring to preach the trinity of individualism, self-reliance, and limited government rather than a gospel of religiosity.

> This again will be . . . a Nation where all who can will be self-reliant. . . . Our towns and our cities, then our counties, then our states, then our regional compacts—and only then, the national government. That, let me remind you, is the ladder of liberty, built by decentralized power. . . . This is a Party. This Republican Party is a Party for free men, not for blind followers, and not for conformists.
>
> In fact, in 1858 Abraham Lincoln said this of the Republican party—and I quote him, because he probably could have said it during the last week or so: "It was composed of strange, discordant, and even hostile elements."

The use of Lincoln quotes in Republican speeches is common. What was odd about Goldwater's use of Lincoln was that he had used Lincoln "the unifier" as a way of celebrating his contrarian style. The muscularity of Goldwater's language represented a rhetorical break from the patricianly style more in keeping with the moderate and liberal Republicans of the era. But it was Goldwater's tough and defiant tone that ultimately ushered in a leaner, some would say meaner, way for conservatives to communicate. Even as he attempts to win over voters, startlingly, Goldwater seems to be saying that he could care less whether voters support him. As he puts it, "Anyone who joins us in all sincerity, we welcome. Those who don't care for our cause, we don't expect to enter our ranks in any case."

And that's when, nearing the end of his address, the former fighter pilot dropped the rhetorical bomb by which his address would forever be remembered:

> *And let our Republicanism, so focused and so dedicated, not be made fuzzy and futile by unthinking and stupid labels. I would remind you that extremism in the defense of liberty is no vice. And let me remind you also that moderation in the pursuit of justice is no virtue.*

The famous line—"extremism in the defense of liberty is no vice"—had actually been the first half of an antithesis, a rhetorical device that juxtaposes antonyms. The opposing words were supposed to be *extremism* in the first sentence and *moderation* in the second. But the roof-raising applause Goldwater received from the first half of his antithesis not only ruined the effect of the device but also altered its meaning. "Moderation in the pursuit of justice is no virtue" was supposed to balance and soften the erstwhile applause line. But the softer second sentence had been swallowed by the tidal wave of excitement from Goldwater's defense of extremism. Watching the raucous Republican response to Goldwater's ode to extremism, one reporter said, "My God, he's going to run as Barry Goldwater."[26] The candidate had actually spoken the word his critics had applied to him—extreme—which only cemented the media in framing Goldwater as an unhinged radical who was far removed from the political mainstream.

The media weren't the only ones alarmed by Goldwater's red-meat conservative declaration, however. Republican moderates such as former president Dwight D. Eisenhower were troubled by the "extremism" line. So much so, in fact, that Ike called for Goldwater to visit his suite at the Fairmont Hotel the morning after the speech to explain just what the former air force pilot had meant. Eisenhower told Goldwater that he had already received word that the controversial line was receiving widespread negative reaction and wasn't playing well in media reports. "Mr. President," Goldwater replied, "when you landed your troops in Normandy, it was an exceedingly extreme action taken because you were committed to the defense of freedom." When Goldwater said this, "Ike's face broke into that inimitable grin. 'I guess you're right, Goldwater. I never thought of it that way.'"[27]

In losing the presidency, Goldwater won a victory for the American conservative movement. His words became ideological kindling that fueled future Republican prairie fires. By galvanizing and inspiring a conservative core constituency, Goldwater transformed myriad Republicans into dyed-in-the-wool conservatives. Indeed, many of today's leaders in the conservative movement began as Goldwaterites. This development, however, was not without short- and long-term negative political consequences. Goldwater went on to suffer one of the most devastating presidential defeats in U.S. history. The 1964 Republican presidential campaign and its resulting lopsided and unfair media coverage destroyed the remaining vestiges of black Republican support. But it was Barry Goldwater whose candidacy put in place the political machinery necessary for conservatism's "Greatest Communicator," who would eventually usher in the Reagan Revolution.

7

Richard M. Nixon

The Beginning of the End

"Checkers"

SEPTEMBER 23, 1952

U.S. CAPITOL, WASHINGTON, D.C.

---

*And you know, the kids, like all kids, love the dog, and
I just want to say this, right now, that regardless of what
they say about it, we're gonna keep it.*

—Richard M. Nixon

During presidential campaigns, media often preface major speeches with the ubiquitous and somewhat hyperbolic phrase "the most important speech of the candidate's political career." One could respond, "But isn't *every* speech 'the most important speech of the candidate's political career?'" True enough. One bad move and a candidate's electoral house of cards can come crashing down. But on September 23, 1952, for Richard Milhous Nixon, the oft-stated comment wasn't an overstatement, it was an understatement. The speech he delivered was decisive. If Nixon's speech had gone badly, U.S. history, as well as GOP history, would have turned out differently—very differently.

In 1952, General Dwight D. Eisenhower had tapped then California senator Richard Nixon to be his vice presidential running mate on the Republican presidential ticket. After it was later revealed that Senator Nixon had an $18,000 personal fund—his opponents and critics called it a secret "slush fund"—Democratic National Committee

(DNC) chairman Stephen A. Mitchell called on Nixon to resign as his party's vice presidential nominee. Mitchell then snidely added that those who couldn't afford to be in politics should not enter politics.[1]

Ike pondered what to do. On the one hand, having a cloud of ethical impropriety hovering over his candidacy was hardly preferable. On the other hand, Nixon enjoyed enormous support from segments of the Republican Party, many of whom were urging Eisenhower to keep Nixon on the ticket. To do otherwise, they argued, would be an act of disloyalty and a sign of weakness. Even Eisenhower's campaign advisers were divided. When several newspapers quickly jumped on the "dump Nixon" bandwagon, many conservative Republicans dug in their heels. If the liberal newspapers were against keeping Nixon, they figured, then he *must* be the right man for vice president.

That's when Robert Humphreys, the chief assistant to Republican National Committee (RNC) chairman Arthur Summerfield, came up with the idea to have Nixon, a Duke University–trained lawyer, take his case directly to the American people. Communication scholar Celeste Michelle Condit notes that 1952 was the year television emerged as the dominant mode of communication in electoral politics. "In 1952, the Presidential candidates spent $11 million; in 1960 they spent $25 million (up 46 percent from 1956), and in 1968, they spent $60 million on television time alone."[2]

Buying airtime for Nixon's self-defense to the nation would cost the RNC almost four times as much money ($75,000) as was in Nixon's disputed fund. Leading up to Nixon's televised speech, General Eisenhower had not decided whether he would publicly state his support for Nixon. Ike told Nixon that after he delivered his speech to the nation, an Ike endorsement might not even be necessary. Frustrated, Nixon told him, "General, a time comes in politics when you have to shit or get off the pot!" Eisenhower simply replied, "Keep your chin up."[3]

The scene had been set. Nixon would deliver his apologia from the El Capitan Theater in Hollywood. With television still in its infancy, the event swept the nation with anticipation. An estimated sixty million Americans tuned in to watch Nixon fight for his political life. Just as the embattled candidate and his wife, Pat, prepared to leave their hotel for the studio, Nixon received a phone call. Top Eisenhower advisers wanted the young California senator to say that while there had been no wrongdoing, he would withdraw his name from the ticket. They wanted him to fall on his sword. Nixon exploded. "Just tell them that I haven't the slightest idea as to what I am going to do and if they want to find out they'd better listen to the broadcast. And tell them I know something about politics too!" Nixon barked.[4]

The television studio set had been stiffly staged, complete with a desk from which Nixon delivered much of the speech before getting up from his chair and standing. Pat Nixon, who had herself done a little acting earlier in her life, sat with a smile cemented on her face. She looked lovely and porcelain, as if she were a stage prop. But just as Hollywood special effects of fifty years ago look different to modern audiences than those who originally viewed them, so, too, must one assume Nixon's performance appeared less scripted to his original viewers than to modern ones. As will be shown, ample evidence exists that the pre–Watergate audience to whom he spoke was convinced. Indeed, Nixon's performance would produce something rare in politics: it would instantly change the course of campaign history and, by extension, the shape of U.S. history from that point forward. As Karlyn Kohrs Campbell and Kathleen Hall Jamieson wrote, Nixon's "Checkers" speech was about to become "the most famous and successful personal apologia in U.S. political history."[5]

> *My Fellow Americans,*
>
> *I come before you tonight as a candidate for the Vice Presidency and as a man whose honesty and integrity has been questioned. . . . I have a theory, too, that the best and only answer to a smear or to an honest misunderstanding of the facts is to tell the truth. And that's why I am here tonight. I want to tell you my side of the case. I'm sure that you have read the charge, and you've heard it, that I, Senator Nixon, took $18,000 from a*

*group of my supporters. . . . And now to answer those questions
let me say this: not one cent of the $18,000 or any other money
of that type ever went to me for my personal use. Every penny
of it was used to pay for political expenses that I did not think
should be charged to the taxpayers of the United States. It was
not a secret fund.*

Right out of the chute Nixon stressed to his listeners that he had
come to face the facts, to tell "his side of the case." Ancient rhetoricians
like Cicero and Aristotle believed that a speaker's character, his ethos,
was the single most important ingredient of persuasive communication.
If the speaker could not be trusted or believed, audiences would fail to
be persuaded. In his first sentence, Nixon stated that his "honesty and
integrity has been questioned." Like a lawyer building his case, the rest
of Nixon's address compiles evidence, both literal and impressionistic,
that reveals he is a common man who has been wrongly accused by
political rivals with personal motives.

*Well, then, some of you will say, and rightly, "Well, what did you
use the fund for, Senator? Why did you have to have it?" . . . The
purpose of the fund simply was to defray political expenses that
I did not feel should be charged to the Government. . . . Well,
then the question arises, you say, "Well, how do you pay for these
and how can you do it legally?" . . . The first way is to be a rich
man. I don't happen to be a rich man, so I couldn't use that one.
Another way that is used is to put your wife on the pay roll.
Let me say, incidentally, that my opponent, my opposite number for the Vice Presidency on the Democratic ticket, does have
his wife on the pay roll and has had her on his pay roll for the
past ten years. Now let me just say this: That's his business, and
I'm not critical of him for doing that. You will have to pass judgment on that particular point. . . .*

*And so I felt that the best way to handle these necessary
political expenses of getting my message to the American peo-*

ple and the speeches I made—the speeches I had printed for the most part concerned this one message of exposing this Administration, the Communism in it, the corruption in it—the only way that I could do that was to accept the aid which people in my home State of California, who contributed to my campaign and who continued to make these contributions after I was elected, were glad to make.

Far from looking like he was "on the take," Nixon painted the portrait of a selfless public servant. Republicans had long battled the stigma of being the party of the rich, but Nixon's declaration that he was a man of modest means rang true. He had grown up painfully poor. Nixon's father had been forced to quit school by the sixth grade, and his Quaker mother had been a woman of humble means and spirit. Historians and others offer psychoanalytic hypotheses as to the insecurities and feelings of inferiority or paranoia that Nixon's impoverished origins may have produced within him. But in his speech, Nixon used the theme of thrift as a way of connecting with the millions of everyday Americans who were watching the broadcast. He was one of them, he seemed to be saying. Unlike the stereotype of the corporate Republican tycoon, he was a Republican with whom they could identify, a theme he returned to throughout his apologia.[6]

Better still, Nixon portrayed himself as the polar opposite of his vice presidential counterpart on the Democratic side, Alabama senator John J. Sparkman. Nixon eagerly pointed out that Sparkman's wife was on the federal payroll. He then ran through an exhaustive list of seemingly every receipt, investment, and asset he ever owned. The net effect of this approach was that Nixon left Americans with the impression that he had nothing to hide, that this was much ado about nothing. Indeed, in delivering his laundry list of small numbers and dollar amounts, he had effectively numbed his audience into believing he was innocent. "How could he possibly have done something wrong financially?" the audience was left thinking. "He didn't get rich, and he didn't even have that much to begin with!"

But all this paled in comparison to Senator Nixon's skillful use of the ultimate symbol of American populism: the family dog. In the following passage, Nixon employs the illustration that gave his speech its name:

> *Well, that's about it. That's what we have. And that's what we owe. It isn't very much. But Pat and I have the satisfaction that every dime that we've got is honestly ours. I should say this, that Pat doesn't have a mink coat. But she does have a respectable Republican cloth coat, and I always tell her she'd look good in anything.*
>
> *One other thing I probably should tell you, because if I don't they'll probably be saying this about me, too. We did get something, a gift, after the election. A man down in Texas heard Pat on the radio mention the fact that our two youngsters would like to have a dog. And believe it or not, the day before we left on this campaign trip we got a message from Union Station in Baltimore, saying they had a package for us. We went down to get it. You know what it was? It was a little cocker spaniel dog, in a crate that he had sent all the way from Texas, black and white, spotted, and our little girl Tricia, the six year old, named it Checkers. And you know, the kids, like all kids, love the dog, and I just want to say this, right now, that regardless of what they say about it, we're gonna keep it.*

In case the listener had forgotten, Nixon again reminded his audience that he and his wife were of modest means and thus unable to afford luxury goods, such as mink coats. By labeling Pat's coat a "respectable Republican cloth coat," the vice presidential candidate transformed the closets of America into a partisan affair. (One wonders whether Democratic owners of cloth coats thought twice about wearing them in the wake of Nixon's address.)

But it was Nixon's recounting of how the family had acquired its beloved Checkers that had stolen the show and warmed listeners to the young California senator. The playfully defiant last line of the passage—"regardless of what they say about it, we're gonna keep it"—came across as lighthearted and fatherly. Liberal communication professor Thomas B. Farrell once humorously quipped that "Richard Nixon would have eaten Checkers smothered in barbecue sauce if it would have helped him become Vice President."[7] But the brooding, paranoid, Machiavellian Watergate Nixon was nowhere to be found in this speech. Instead, Americans had seen a self-made man with a loving wife divulging his entire financial history to the nation and talking about the family pet. The invocation of the family dog had been a stroke of rhetorical brilliance. Not only had it humanized the candidate, it invited a subtle form of disgust in the listener as well. "How could anyone make political hay out of a little girl's puppy dog?" listeners might respond.

Using a politician's dog to shame his opponents was not without precedent. Indeed, Nixon's Checkers device had an unlikely origin: President Franklin Delano Roosevelt. During the 1944 presidential election, word had spread that President Roosevelt may have sent a battleship to retrieve his little Scottish terrier, Fala, from the Aleutian Islands. Such a tale, if proven true (it wasn't), would have demonstrated an imperious attitude and a gross misuse of taxpayer money. Wisely, FDR used the story to his advantage: "These Republican leaders have not been content with attacks on me, or on my wife, or on my sons. No, not content with that. They now include my little dog, Fala."[8] By using humor to deflect criticism of perceived personal misconduct, Nixon had followed in FDR's footsteps.

> *It isn't easy to come before a nationwide audience and bare your life, as I've done. . . . Mr. Mitchell, the Chairman of the Democratic National Committee, made this statement that if a man couldn't afford to be in the United States Senate, he shouldn't run for the Senate. And I just want to make my position clear. I don't agree with Mr. Mitchell when he says that only a rich man should serve his Government in the United States Senate or in the Congress. I don't believe that represents the thinking*

of the Democratic Party, and I know that it doesn't represent the thinking of the Republican Party.

I believe that it's fine that a man like Governor Stevenson, who inherited a fortune from his father, can run for President. But I also feel that it's essential in this country of ours that a man of modest means can also run for President, because, you know, remember Abraham Lincoln, you remember what he said: "God must have loved the common people—he made so many of them."

With his Republican viewing audience now on his side, Nixon further contrasted himself from the opposing party's political ticket by reminding listeners that Illinois governor Adlai Stevenson, the Democratic nominee for president, had *inherited* his wealth. Nixon then landed a devastating blow against the man who had made an elitist jab about only men who could "afford" it running for politics, DNC chairman Stephen A. Mitchell. Nixon's Lincoln quote, intended to resonate with his Republican target audience, had merely been the icing on the populist cake. As historian Herbert S. Parmet wrote, while "a contemptuous minority derided the speech as the unctuous performance of a Uriah Heep," most Americans viewed Nixon like "a figure from a Frank Capra movie, a 'Mr. Smith' who had gone to Washington and found himself contending with all the problems that the Mr. Smiths of America could recognize."[9]

Now let me say this: I know that this is not the last of the smears. In spite of my explanation tonight, other smears will be made. . . .

And now, finally, I know that you wonder whether or not I am going to stay on the Republican ticket or resign. Let me say this: I don't believe that I ought to quit, because I'm not a quitter. And, incidentally, Pat's not a quitter. After all, her name is Patricia Ryan and she was born on St. Patrick's Day, and you know the Irish never quit. But the decision, my friends, is not mine. I would do nothing that would harm the possibilities of Dwight Eisenhower to become President of the United States. And for that reason I am submitting to the Republican National Committee tonight through this television broadcast the decision which it is theirs to make. Let them decide whether my position on the ticket will help or hurt. And I am going to ask you to help them decide. Wire and write the Republican National Committee whether you think I should stay on or whether I should get off. And whatever their decision is, I will abide by it.

But just let me say this last word. Regardless of what happens, I'm going to continue this fight. I'm going to campaign up and down in America until we drive the crooks and the Communists and those that defend them out of Washington. And remember folks, Eisenhower is a great man, believe me. He's a great man. And a vote for Eisenhower is a vote for what's good for America.

The broadcast ended before Nixon had been able to give viewers the RNC's mailing address. But this had the unexpected consequence of multiplying the efforts viewers made to contact Republican sources. The results were unprecedented. Telephone systems in San Francisco were flooded with so many calls that they were nearly shut down.[10] An astounding three hundred thousand letters and telegrams poured into the RNC, two million messages in total, 350 to 1 in favor of Nixon staying on the ticket. A total of $62,000 in campaign contributions had been stuffed into the letters of support, almost enough to cover the airtime the RNC had purchased.[11] Even today, Nixon's "Checkers" speech remains *the* model for political apologias.[12]

Richard Nixon's "Checkers" address had been a watershed event for the candidate, the Republican Party, and the nation. As Humphreys later wrote in his private notes, had Nixon been dropped from the ticket, "the whole future of American politics would have been different . . . Ike would have lost the election. Ike, himself, thought so; . . . Nixon never would have been Vice President. He never would have been able to run for President in 1960. He never would have been able to run again in 1968."[13]

Nor, one might add, would he have been able to resign in disgrace on August 8, 1974, in the wake of the Watergate scandal that gripped the nation. Indeed, Gerald R. Ford would inherit a deeply wounded Republican Party and an America whose spirit had been broken.

— 8 —

Gerald R. Ford

"Our Long National Nightmare Is Over"

Oath of the U.S. Presidency

AUGUST 9, 1974

EAST ROOM OF THE WHITE HOUSE, WASHINGTON, D.C.

---

*I am acutely aware that you have not elected me as your
President by your ballots, so I ask you to confirm me as your
President with your prayers.*

—Gerald R. Ford

The Roman rhetorician Quintilian once famously said that the goal
of rhetoric (persuasion) is to become "the good man speaking well."
Gerald Rudolph Ford is roundly regarded as having been the former, but he is seldom accused of having done the latter. Ford
speechwriter Craig R. Smith put it this way: "In Gerald Ford's case,
his verbal stumbling, combined with his pardon of Richard Nixon,
nearly destroyed his presidency."[1] Smith notes that besides delivering public speeches at Yale Law School, Ford possessed little in the
way of oratorical training. While he might have been perfectly at
home in front of a crowd of eighty thousand screaming University
of Michigan football fans, Ford became awkward in front of an audience of listeners.

Still, Ford's background as a star football player was not without its
political utility. He had learned how to enter the game under pressure and how to excel in the clutch. So perhaps it is fitting that President Ford's most famous and influential oration came during just

such a moment. With the help of Bob Hartmann, his old friend and vice presidential chief of staff, Ford crafted a speech that achieved what ancient public speakers referred to as Kairos (the right or opportune moment) and To Prepon (the fitting or appropriate message). Put another way, Ford's speech delivered the right message at the right moment. In so doing, as Smith noted, "Ford's desire to be honest and forthright would for a time overcome his sometimes inarticulate nature."[2]

Gerald Ford remains the first and only chief executive who was never elected to become president or vice president. The extraordinary circumstances of his 895-day presidency were without precedent.[3] Growing up in Grand Rapids, Michigan, Ford learned the art of adaptation and of rolling with adversity. It wasn't until he was a teenager that he discovered that the man he had believed to be his father, Gerald Rudolf Ford, was actually his stepfather who had adopted him and given him his own name.[4] As presidential historian Fred I. Greenstein notes, Ford's belief in hard work and responsibility allowed him to press on, first as an Eagle Scout and honors student, and then as a star University of Michigan football player who had received an athletic scholarship. Even when he had been offered a chance to play professional football, he rejected the offer as a distraction that "wouldn't lead me anywhere."[5] He later graduated from Yale Law School, practiced law, and then served twenty-five years in the U.S. House of Representatives. What he lacked in style he made up for in substance. Dependability and decency were his two great assets. "I'm a Ford, not a Lincoln," his campaign slogan proclaimed.

But many felt Ford's brand of midwestern humility and pragmatic style were precisely what was needed in Watergate's aftermath. A man of greater hubris would not have sufficed. Such a leader would not have exhibited the humility necessary to bind up the nation's wounds and heal a crippled country. Thus, when Ford was preparing the address for his oath-taking (an inaugural address it was not), he and Hartmann had gone to great lengths to make sure that the words were

To Prepon, that they did not in any way overreach or assert a mandate that did not exist. He would speak humbly.

Still, Ford had other constraints with which to deal and objectives to achieve. First, he needed to assure the nation that his elevation to president of the United States had not been the result of some back-channel deal or lust for power. Second, he needed to remind Americans that despite the unusual circumstances of his presidential selection, he would nevertheless have full constitutional powers as the chief executive. Third, he needed to unite Americans who had waged a bitter partisan war against one another to move forward for the good of the nation. Fourth, he needed to recognize the blight that was Watergate. And finally, unlike past vice presidents who had succeeded their predecessors, Ford needed to distance himself from Richard Nixon while simultaneously bestowing national forgiveness on the disgraced president for his sins against the Constitution and country. It was a lot to accomplish.

Mr. Chief Justice, my dear friends, my fellow Americans:

The oath that I have taken is the same oath that was taken by George Washington and by every President under the Constitution. But I assume the Presidency under extraordinary circumstances never before experienced by Americans. This is an hour of history that troubles our minds and hurts our hearts.

Therefore, I feel it is my first duty to make an unprecedented compact with my countrymen. Not an inaugural address, not a fireside chat, not a campaign speech—just a little straight talk among friends. And I intend it to be the first of many.

I am acutely aware that you have not elected me as your President by your ballots, and so I ask you to confirm me as your President with your prayers. And I hope that such prayers will also be the first of many. If you have not chosen me by secret ballot, neither have I gained office by any secret promises. I have not campaigned either for the Presidency or the Vice Presidency. I have not subscribed to any partisan platform. I am indebted to no man, and only to one woman—my dear wife—as I begin this very difficult job.

I have not sought this enormous responsibility, but I will not shirk it. Those who nominated and confirmed me as Vice President were my friends and are my friends. They were of both parties, elected by all the people and acting under the Constitution in their name. It is only fitting then that I should pledge to them and to you that I will be the President of all the people.

Thomas Jefferson said the people are the only sure reliance for the preservation of our liberty. And down the years, Abraham Lincoln renewed this American article of faith asking, "Is there any better way or equal hope in the world?" . . . We cannot stand still or slip backwards. We must go forward now together. . . . I believe that truth is the glue that holds government together, not only our Government but civilization itself. That bond, though strained, is unbroken at home and abroad.

In all my public and private acts as your President, I expect to follow my instincts of openness and candor with full confidence that honesty is always the best policy in the end.

My fellow Americans, our long national nightmare is over.

Our Constitution works. Our great Republic is a government of laws and not of men. Here, the people rule. But there is a higher Power, by whatever name we honor Him, who ordains not only righteousness but love, not only justice but mercy. As we bind up the internal wounds of Watergate, more painful and more poisonous than those of foreign wars, let us restore the golden rule to our political process, and let brotherly love purge our hearts of suspicion and of hate.

In the beginning, I asked you to pray for me. Before closing, I ask again your prayers, for Richard Nixon and for his family. May our former President, who brought peace to millions, find it for himself. May God bless and comfort his wonderful wife and daughters, whose love and loyalty will forever be a shining legacy to all who bear the lonely burdens of the White House. I can only guess at those burdens, although I have witnessed at close hand the tragedies that befell three Presidents and the lesser trials of others.

With all the strength and all the good sense I have gained from life, with all the confidence my family, my friends, and my dedicated staff impart to me, and with the good will of countless Americans I have encountered in recent visits to 40 States, I now solemnly reaffirm my promise I made to you last December 6: To uphold the Constitution; to do what is right as God gives me to see the right; and to do the very best I can for America.

God helping me, I will not let you down.

Thank you.

The tone had been conversational, colloquial even. He had spoken of national unity as "glue," he had asked more than once for people to pray for him, and he recognized that he was a proxy president, a "fill in" that had not been elected by the will of the people. But Ford punctuated the "long national nightmare" with hope and goodness. He seemed reasonable, honest, and decent—precisely the qualities the nation needed to see and feel in a leader. Most important of all, he achieved the necessary objectives he needed to cover in his speech and thereby neutralized the myriad rhetorical exigencies that surrounded him.

The following month, however, he sealed his electoral fate when he announced that he would preemptively pardon Nixon. Some viewed his decision as evidence of wrongdoing, a sign that he had brokered a deal. To others, it was yet another reminder of Ford's selfless nature and willingness to put national healing above self-preservation. As historian Steven Hayward wrote, "It was a supreme and necessary act of mercy, which even Nixon-hating liberals have come over time to admit. But the timing was awkward for Ford. 'Will there ever be a right time?' Ford asked when his aides second-guessed him."[6]

Yet from whatever vantage point one viewed the decision, President Ford's oath of the U.S. presidency had stanched the national bleeding. He had found the right words, just when the United States needed them most.

Ronald Reagan

A Shining Speaker on a Hill

"The Evil Empire"

---

*The real crisis we face today is a spiritual one; at root,
it is a test of moral will and faith.*

—Ronald Reagan

It wasn't supposed to be a big speech. In fact, so perfunctory had President Reagan's March 8, 1983, speech to the annual convention of the National Association of Evangelicals in Orlando, Florida, been that there is but one amateur video recording of its delivery, and even that is missing the final seven minutes of the address (the videographer ran out of tape). The audience was small by presidential standards, a mere two thousand or so persons. But the minute it was learned that President Reagan had referred to the Soviet Union as an "evil empire," word blazed through American and international media like a fireball. If this was the way Reagan practiced diplomacy, his critics trembled to think how he would speak in a moment of international friction.

Yet, all this proved was that the president's critics never understood his rhetorical strategy. In their eyes, President Reagan's strident rhetoric against the Soviet Union—a Communist regime responsible for the slaughter and imprisonment of tens of millions during its murderous reign—was further evidence that Reagan was a reckless cowboy, an unhinged demagogue who lacked the intellectual equipment necessary to communicate in a civil and diplomatic tone. But what they had construed as name-calling, Reagan understood to be a crucial component of winning the Cold War. Using words like wrecking balls, Reagan sought to demolish the wall of Soviet lies and deceptions that others had turned a blind eye toward. He called Soviet Communism evil.

Berkeley political science professor and former vice presidential speechwriter William Ker Muir Jr. contends that the Reagan presidency used the word *evil* to reinvigorate "the national discourse, thereby affirming moral freedom."[1] Reagan had rejected moral relativism all his life. In his view, there was good and there was evil, period. This view made his detractors cringe. How could someone be so myopic, so pedestrian in his thinking, they groused.

The issue is so much more complicated and nuanced; it's not black and white. Case in point: reporter Sam Donaldson, who had been in the audience in the Citrus Crown Ballroom at the Orlando Sheraton Twin Towers Hotel where Reagan spoke. When Reagan uttered the phrase "evil empire," one observer recalled that "the most unbelievable smirk" spread across Donaldson's face.[2]

But the speechwriter who had penned the speech, Pulitzer prize–winner Tony Dolan, understood Reagan's deepest philosophies and beliefs, as well as his rhetorical patterns and preferences. Dolan says that Reagan never suffered from "the moral uncertainty, the anomie, that tended to arrest decisive action."[3] Muir notes that it was Reagan and Dolan's belief that "the lack of language to make important distinctions undermined strong convictions."[4] Hence, the "evil empire."

What is most remarkable about Reagan's "evil empire" speech is that today it is largely assumed to have been a foreign policy address aimed at tamping down Christians' possible slow creep toward the nuclear freeze proposal. But the first half of the speech had been about what Reagan considered to be the evil endemic to the United States' history of slavery, as well as its present manifestations of evil, namely abortion. Ironically enough, then, the power phrase that had garnered so much attention, "evil empire," deflected attention away from what some of his liberal critics might have considered even more provocative and uncouth: a sitting president declaring that "[t]here is sin and evil in the world, and we're enjoined by Scripture and the Lord Jesus to oppose it with all our might." True to the Reagan style, if his critics didn't like his bold proclamations of faith and condemnation of evil, tough. He knew the vast majority of Americans were and would remain with him. So he spoke:

> *I want you to know that this administration is motivated by a political philosophy that sees the greatness of America in you, her people, and in your families, churches, neighborhoods, communities. . . . Now, I don't have to tell you that this puts us in opposition to, or at least out of step with, a prevailing attitude of many who have turned to a modern-day secularism, discarding the tried and time-tested values upon which our very civilization is based. No matter how well intentioned, their value system is radically different from that of most Americans.*
>
> *Sometimes their voices are louder than ours, but they are not yet a majority.*

Reagan's message of being ostracized and ridiculed for one's beliefs was right at home with the Evangelical audience to which he spoke. One of the core principles of Evangelical Christianity holds that, as stated in Matthew 7:13–14, "Enter through the narrow gate. For wide is the gate and broad is the road that leads to destruction, and many enter through it. But small is the gate and narrow the road that leads to life, and only a few find it." Elsewhere in the New Testament, Christians are encouraged numerous times to be "the salt of the world," meaning to preserve, or conserve (as in conservative), the values that lead toward more Godly living, even in the face of persecution and ridicule. In this way, secular mockery becomes a badge of faith, a sign of obedience to God's will. And it was Reagan's embedding of Christian doctrine into his words that gave them their resonance with Christian Americans:

Let me state the case as briefly and simply as I can. An organization of citizens, sincerely motivated, deeply concerned about the increase in illegitimate births and abortions involving girls well below the age of consent, some time ago established a nationwide network of clinics to offer help to these girls and, hopefully, alleviate this situation. Now, again, let me say, I do not fault their intent. However, in their well-intentioned effort, these clinics decided to provide advice and birth control drugs and devices to underage girls without the knowledge of their parents.

For some years now, the federal government has helped with funds to subsidize these clinics. In providing for this, the Congress decreed that every effort would be made to maximize parental participation. Nevertheless, the drugs and devices are prescribed without getting parental consent or giving notification after they've done so. Girls termed "sexually active"—and that has replaced the word "promiscuous"—are given this help in order to prevent illegitimate birth or abortion.

Well, we have ordered clinics receiving federal funds to notify the parents such help has been given . . . but no one seems to mention morality as playing a part in the subject of sex.

Is all of Judeo-Christian tradition wrong? Are we to believe that something so sacred can be looked upon as a purely physical thing with no potential for emotional and psychological harm? And isn't it the parents' right to give counsel and advice to keep their children from making mistakes that may affect their entire lives?

Many of us in government would like to know what parents think about this intrusion in their family by government. We're going to fight in the courts. The right of parents and the rights of family take precedence over those of Washington-based bureaucrats and social engineers.

Here again, Reagan displayed that he understood the values and beliefs of his audience and that he respected those values enough to stand up and fight for the things his audience held most dear.

> *But the fight against parental notification is really only one example of many attempts to water down traditional values and even abrogate the original terms of American democracy. Freedom prospers when religion is vibrant and the rule of law under God is acknowledged. When our Founding Fathers passed the First Amendment, they sought to protect churches from government interference. They never intended to construct a wall of hostility between government and the concept of religious belief itself.*
>
> *The evidence of this permeates our history and our government. The Declaration of Independence mentions the Supreme Being no less than four times. "In God We Trust" is engraved on our coinage. The Supreme Court opens its proceedings with a religious invocation. And the members of Congress open their sessions with a prayer. I just happen to believe the schoolchildren of the United States are entitled to the same privileges as Supreme Court justices and congressmen.*
>
> *Last year, I sent the Congress a constitutional amendment to restore prayer to public schools. Already this session, there's growing bipartisan support for the amendment, and I am calling on the Congress to act speedily to pass it and to let our children pray. . . .*
>
> *More than a decade ago, a Supreme Court decision literally wiped off the books of fifty states statutes protecting the rights of unborn children. Abortion on demand now takes the lives of up to one and a half million unborn children a year. Human life legislation ending this tragedy will someday pass the Congress, and you and I must never rest until it does. Unless and until it can be proven that the unborn child is not a living entity, then its right to life, liberty, and the pursuit of happiness must be protected. . . .*

But we must never forget that no government schemes are going to perfect man. We know that living in this world means dealing with what philosophers would call the phenomenology of evil or, as theologians would put it, the doctrine of sin. There is sin and evil in the world, and we're enjoined by Scripture and the Lord Jesus to oppose it with all our might. Our nation, too, has a legacy of evil with which it must deal. The glory of this land has been its capacity for transcending the moral evils of our past. For example, the long struggle of minority citizens for equal rights, once a source of disunity and civil war is now a point of pride for all Americans. We must never go back. There is no room for racism, anti-Semitism, or other forms of ethnic and racial hatred in this country.

Parental notification, abortion, "In God We Trust" on the coinage, school prayer—interestingly, these issues remain at the forefront of the culture wars more than two decades after Reagan delivered his speech. But before Reagan could declare the Soviet Union an "evil empire," he needed to inoculate his argument from charges of hypocrisy by first recognizing the American blight of slavery that Abraham Lincoln had equated with the most sinister of sins, a form of depravity that would require national cleansing and spiritual "rebirth."

They must be made to understand we will never compromise our principles and standards. We will never give away our freedom. We will never abandon our belief in God. And we will never stop searching for a genuine peace. But we can assure none of these things America stands for through the so-called nuclear freeze solutions proposed by some.

The truth is that a freeze now would be a very dangerous fraud, for that is merely the illusion of peace. The reality is that we must find peace through strength. . . . A number of years ago, I heard a young father, a very prominent young man in the enter-

tainment world, addressing a tremendous gathering in California. It was during the time of the cold war, and communism and our own way of life were very much on people's minds. And he was speaking to that subject. And suddenly, though, I heard him saying, "I love my little girls more than anything." And I said to myself, "Oh, no, don't. You can't—don't say that." But I had underestimated him. He went on: "I would rather see my little girls die now; still believing in God, than have them grow up under communism and one day die no longer believing in God."

There were thousands of young people in that audience. They came to their feet with shouts of joy. They had instantly recognized the profound truth in what he had said, with regard to the physical and the soul and what was truly important. Yes, let us pray for the salvation of all of those who live in that totalitarian darkness. Pray they will discover the joy of knowing God. But until they do, let us be aware that while they preach the supremacy of the State, declare its omnipotence over individual man, and predict its eventual domination of all peoples on the earth, they are the focus of evil in the modern world.

It was C. S. Lewis who, in his unforgettable Screwtape Letters, wrote: "The greatest evil is not done now in those sordid 'dens of crime' that Dickens loved to paint. It is not even done in concentration camps and labor camps. In those we see its final result. But it is conceived and ordered; moved, seconded, carried and minuted in clear, carpeted, warmed, and well-lighted offices, by quiet men with white collars and cut fingernails and smooth-shaven cheeks who do not need to raise their voice."

. . . If history teaches anything, it teaches that simpleminded appeasement or wishful thinking about our adversaries is folly. It means the betrayal of our past, the squandering of our freedom. . . .

So, in your discussions of the nuclear freeze proposals, I urge you to beware the temptation of pride—the temptation of blithely declaring yourselves above it all and label both sides equally at fault, to ignore the facts of history and the aggressive impulses of an evil empire, to simply call the arms race a giant misunderstanding and thereby remove yourself from the struggle between right and wrong and good and evil. . . .

The real crisis we face today is a spiritual one; at root, it is a test of moral will and faith.

Reagan had pivoted from what he saw as the domestic instances of evil, such as suppression of prayer in schools and abortion, into the foreign policy evils that were codified in the symbol of Soviet totalitarianism. Again, Reagan returns to the Christian rhetorical well. The president's gripping account of the father who would "rather see my little girls die now, still believing in God, than have them grow up under communism and one day die no longer believing in God" had actually been a reference to comments made by Pat Boone.[5] But they had further underscored the "narrow gate" and "salt of the world" dynamics laid out earlier in the speech; Christians, the president argued, were to view the world differently from nonbelievers and thus understood that the battle between democracy and Communism was just another way of saying that Christian Americans were in a war against atheist Soviet domination. Hence, his strong declaration that "[w]e will never abandon our belief in God."

Reagan's citation of C. S. Lewis's best-selling Christian book *The Screwtape Letters* further underscores just how well he understood and related with his primary target audience. Lewis's book is written from the perspective of a demon that has been tasked by Satan to "trip up" a Christian on earth. As the president's illustration suggests, one of the dominant lessons of the book is that sin seldom announces itself wearing a devil's tail and clutching a pitchfork; rather, in his craftiness, Satan masks sin so that it appears innocuous and harmless—good even. Reagan is therefore implying that, while seemingly well intentioned, the nuclear freeze movement would merely play into the hands of the "evil empire." Given his daughter Patti Davis's active role in the nuclear freeze movement, Reagan's charge was not only polit-ical, but personal. In this way, the president's admonition not to be "duped" by those who promise peace through disarmament could just as easily apply to his daughter as to the nation.

> *I believe that communism is another sad, bizarre chapter in human history whose last—last pages even now are being writ-ten. . . .For in the words of Isaiah: "He giveth power to the faint; and to them that have no might He increased strength. But they that wait upon the Lord shall renew their strength; they shall mount up with wings as eagles; they shall run, and not be weary."*
>
> *God bless you and thank you very much.*

Although this speech was delivered six years before the collapse of the Berlin Wall, Reagan had boldly declared that Communism's "last pages even now are being written." The line is strikingly prophetic. Still, at the time, it had been the "evil empire" sound bite that had rocked the international and diplomatic arena. While Dolan had writ-ten the speech, Reagan biographer Lou Cannon notes that Reagan's fiercely anti-Communist message "had been much the same when Dolan was a toddler and Reagan was writing his own speeches on three-by-five cards."[6] Dolan agrees. As he saw it, the primary job of a Reagan speechwriter was to plagiarize the president's old speeches and give them back to him to deliver.[7]

Peter Robinson, the Reagan speechwriter who wrote the "tear down this wall" speech at the Brandenberg Gate, remembers the media firestorm that Reagan's "evil empire" address created: "I discov-ered that for months—literally months—I could count on seeing that phrase, 'evil empire,' referred to in a newspaper or magazine at least once or twice a week. *National Review* and the *Wall Street Journal* applauded it. Nearly every other publication denounced it. But the phrase continued to echo."[8]

That echo not only ricocheted around the United States, but it eventually found its way to the darkest and most freedom-starved crevices of human existence: the Russian gulags. Soviet dissident Natan Sharansky had been imprisoned in Permanent Labor Camp 35 in the Urals when word was passed of the "evil empire" speech. Years later, when Reagan's pressure on Russia resulted in Sharansky's release, the former dissident traveled to the United States to visit the White House at President Reagan's request. "I told him that his speech about the Evil Empire was a great encourager for us," said Sharansky. "An American leader was calling a spade a spade. . . . President Reagan understood the nature of a totalitarian regime. He believed freedom is something that belongs to all the people, and if you encourage it and support it you can win."[9]

Indeed, "evil empire" had produced an echo, an echo whose boom pounded against a wall halfway around the globe, prepping it for later demolition.

Challenger

JANUARY 28, 1986

OVAL OFFICE, THE WHITE HOUSE, WASHINGTON, D.C.

We will never forget them, nor the last time we saw them, this morning, as they prepared for their journey and waved goodbye and "slipped the surly bonds of earth" to "touch the face of God."

—Ronald Reagan

On January 28, 1986, at 11:38 a.m., thousands of American school-children sat in front of television screens in anxious anticipation of the event they had been learning about as part of the National Aeronautics and Space Administration (NASA)–produced curriculum titled "Teacher in Space." Over eleven thousand teachers across the country had competed in a competition to become the first teacher in space. Christa McAuliffe had won the contest and was now inside the space shuttle *Challenger* at which the schoolchildren stared.

Seventy-three seconds—that's how long the children had been staring at the arcing space shuttle. At 11:39, *Challenger* exploded in midflight, leaving a Y-shaped scar of smoke across a crystal-blue Florida sky. The seven astronauts inside the spacecraft had been incinerated on live national television. Gasps of horror could be heard from those on the ground watching the launch live; teachers in classrooms calmed confused and scared students. America mourned—and waited.

President Ronald Reagan had been scheduled that evening to deliver his constitutionally required message to the nation in the form of his State of the Union address. Dick Wirthlin, Reagan's chief political strategist and pollster, recalls that the decision to postpone the president's State of the Union had been made quickly.[10] Peggy Noonan, one of Reagan's best speechwriters, had drafted a substitute speech at warp speed. Less than six hours after the *Challenger* exploded, Americans saw their president seated at his desk inside the Oval Office seeming to look through the television screen and into the faces of the millions who had tuned in:

> *Ladies and Gentlemen, I'd planned to speak to you tonight to report on the state of the Union, but the events of earlier today have led me to change those plans. Today is a day for mourning and remembering. Nancy and I are pained to the core by the tragedy of the shuttle* Challenger. *We know we share this pain with all of the people of our country. This is truly a national loss.*
>
> *Nineteen years ago, almost to the day, we lost three astronauts in a terrible accident on the ground. But we've never lost an astronaut in flight. We've never had a tragedy like this. And perhaps we've forgotten the courage it took for the crew of the shuttle. But they, the Challenger Seven, were aware of the dangers, but overcame them and did their jobs brilliantly. We mourn seven heroes: Michael Smith, Dick Scobee, Judith Resnik, Ronald McNair, Ellison Onizuka, Gregory Jarvis, and Christa McAuliffe. We mourn their loss as a nation together. For the families of the seven, we cannot bear, as you do, the full impact of this tragedy. But we feel the loss, and we're thinking about you so very much. Your loved ones were daring and brave, and they had that special grace, that special spirit that says, "Give me a challenge, and I'll meet it with joy." They had a hunger to explore the universe and discover its truths. They wished to serve, and they did. They served all of us.*

Aristotle said that there are three kinds of speeches: deliberative (policy-based) speeches, forensic (legal) speeches, and epideictic (ceremonial) speeches.[11] To this point, the speech appeared to be a traditional eulogy, or epideictic, speech. The president had explained his reason for postponing the state of the Union speech he and his advisers had spent months preparing; he had expressed his and the First Lady's sorrow and sympathy for the families; and he had identified each victim by name. But rhetoric professor Mary E. Stuckey contends that "the *Challenger* speech is not reducible to a predefined type."[12] Instead, as the next passage of the president's speech makes clear, in addition to communicating the nation's sorrow and grief, Reagan had a second objective, this one deliberative:

We've grown used to wonders in this century. It's hard to dazzle us. But for twenty-five years the United States space program has been doing just that. We've grown used to the idea of space, and, perhaps we forget that we've only just begun. We're still pioneers. They, the members of the Challenger *crew, were pioneers.*

And I want to say something to the schoolchildren of America who were watching the live coverage of the shuttle's take-off. I know it's hard to understand, but sometimes painful things like this happen. It's all part of the process of exploration and discovery. It's all part of taking a chance and expanding man's horizons. The future doesn't belong to the fainthearted; it belongs to the brave. The Challenger *crew was pulling us into the future, and we'll continue to follow them.*

I've always had great faith in and respect for our space program. And what happened today does nothing to diminish it. We don't hide our space program. We don't keep secrets and cover things up. We do it all up front and in public. That's the way freedom is, and we wouldn't change it for a minute.

We'll continue our quest in space. There will be more shuttle flights and more shuttle crews and, yes, more volunteers, more civilians, more teachers in space. Nothing ends here; our hopes and our journeys continue.

I want to add that I wish I could talk to every man and woman who works for NASA, or who worked on this mission and tell them: "Your dedication and professionalism have moved and impressed us for decades. And we know of your anguish. We share it."

The president had done something unique among presidential speeches: he had spoken directly to the nation's children. Wirthlin writes, "The *Challenger* tragedy had left American children with big questions and broken hearts. As a father, Reagan could remember how difficult it had been to explain to his daughter Patti why her goldfish weren't swimming. Now millions of American parents would be faced with a task much greater, and he wanted to do what little he could to help them."[13]

In her memoir, Noonan wrote that when she saw *Challenger* explode on television, the seven-year-old daughter of Ben Elliot, one of her colleagues, happened to be in the office that day. The little girl's name was Meredith. Noonan recalls that Meredith's eyes locked on the television as what was left of the shuttle fell back to earth. "The teacher is on it," she said. "Is the teacher all right?"[14]

But Noonan had another form of input to help her formulate the president's message of solace to the thousands of children who had been forced to confront the painful concept of mortality: Ronald Reagan. Karna Small, the assistant to National Security Council director Bud McFarlane, had called shortly after the explosion to notify Noonan that she had taken notes from President Reagan's meeting with network anchors. Among the president's notated answers to reporters' questions, Noonan had seen the following exchange: What can you say to the children to help them understand? "Pioneers have always given their lives on the frontier. The problem is that it's more of a shock to all as we see it happening, not just hear about something miles away— but we must make it clear [to the children] that life goes on."[15]

Reagan's words spoken to American schoolchildren had been an artful fusion of both epideictic and deliberative oratory. On the one hand, he was clearly offering children solace for the painful things that they had witnessed. On the other hand, he was telling children that NASA's mission—indeed, the mission of all exploration—would press on. Reagan's decision to continue his steadfast support for the program had been bolstered by the families of the seven astronauts. In a personal letter written to John Howard, president of the Rockford Institute, just five days after the shuttle tragedy, Reagan stated, "These have been difficult times back here. Meeting with the families as we did was, as you can imagine, an emotional experience, indeed heartbreaking. In phoning them before our meeting, every family said through their tears—the program must be continued."[16] Even though tender in sentiment, Reagan's words were, at base, indicative of a policy position, and thus deliberative. As Mary E. Stuckey has argued, "These two emphases, one epideictic and the other deliberative, guided the entire speech."[17]

> There's a coincidence today. On this day three hundred and ninety years ago, the great explorer Sir Francis Drake died aboard ship off the coast of Panama. In his lifetime the great frontiers were the oceans, and a historian later said, "He lived by the sea, died on it, and was buried in it." Well, today, we can say of the Challenger crew: Their dedication was, like Drake's, complete.
>
> The crew of the space shuttle Challenger honored us by the manner in which they lived their lives. We will never forget them, nor the last time we saw them, this morning, as they prepared for their journey and waved goodbye and "slipped the surly bonds of earth" to "touch the face of God."

Determined not to allow the nation's grief to erode the nation's support for NASA or further space missions, President Reagan's invocation of Sir Francis Drake reminded his audience that risk remains an inherent part of exploration. The message clearly resonated. According to a poll taken by *U.S. News & World Report* just two days after the president's address, 73 percent of those surveyed agreed with the statement that the deaths of the *Challenger* seven were "a regrettable disaster but nevertheless a price we must be willing to pay for the exploration and mastery of space."[18] Ever since *Sputnik* and with the Cold War still raging, maintaining an image of strength had remained a critical component of the U.S. strategy to heap international pressure on the Soviet Union.

But it had been the soaring eloquence of Reagan's final line that secured the speech's place in history as among the "Greatest Communicator's" best orations. Noonan said that the short time she'd had to draft the speech meant that "it went almost as written." Archival records reveal that the speech went through at least three official drafts, but that these were, as Noonan suggests, relatively minor.[19] Ironically, the speech's powerful closing line almost fell victim to the editorial knife. The suggested edit came from a young National Security Council staffer who had told Noonan that the final quote would be much better if she would change it to read, "reach out and touch someone—touch the face of God." Noonan later wrote that "it was the worst edit I received in all my time in the White House," and that the young staffer had "heard it in a commercial."[20] Luckily for Noonan, and the annals of Republican eloquence, she successfully fended off the suggestion.

Reagan loved the inclusion of the quote. It was, of course, a line from the old poem "High Flight" by John Gillespie Magee, with which Reagan had been familiar. Yet even though Noonan had not known this at the time, she said "it was precisely the kind of poem he would have known. . . . It had been popular during the war [World War II]."[21] As stirring as the words were, Reagan's delivery of them was masterful. So powerful, in fact, that the president's *Challenger* eulogy literally made his battle-hardened, partisan foe but personal friend, Speaker of the House "Tip" O'Neill, weep. Indeed, Reagan's words transcended the boundaries of not just time but ideology. Following Reagan's speech, O'Neill came to the conclusion that "with a prepared text he's the best public speaker I've ever seen. . . . I'm beginning to think that in this respect he dwarfs both Roosevelt and Kennedy."[22]

"Mr. Gorbachev, Tear Down This Wall"

JUNE 12, 1987

BRANDENBURG GATE, BERLIN, GERMANY

[T]his wall will fall, for it cannot withstand faith; it cannot withstand truth. The wall cannot withstand freedom.

—Ronald Reagan

When Ronald Reagan arrived in Germany and stood in front of the Berlin Wall for the very first time, his aides recall that his usually cheerful countenance had grown sallow. As he walked closer to survey the vast edifice, those who were with him say he just stood there, awestruck and silent. Then, after absorbing the reality of what Communism had wrought, Reagan turned to speechwriter Peter Hannaford and foreign policy adviser Dick Allen and said, "We have got to find a way to knock this thing down."[23] The date was November 1978.

Nine years later, President Ronald Reagan traveled there once again to deliver his tour de force oration standing before the Brandenburg Gate. Going all the way back to his days in Hollywood and as president of the Screen Actors Guild (1947–1952), Reagan had had it out for Communism and had thrown up obstacles in its path every chance he could. Historian Peter Schweizer recounts the story of Sterling Hayden, an actor and member of the Communist Party.

Hayden confessed during congressional testimony that the Communists had attempted to take over the entertainment unions but had been thwarted in doing so. He said they had been foiled by Reagan, "who was a one-man battalion."[24] Indeed, Reagan's animosity toward Communism was no secret. He was once asked what he thought of the Berlin Wall. "It's as ugly as the idea behind it," Reagan answered.[25]

This was the crux of the matter for Reagan. The Berlin Wall was more than an ugly edifice. It was a rhetorical symbol, a metaphor of all that was evil about Communism. In his autobiography *An American Life*, Reagan expressed his disgust and contempt for the structure. The Berlin Wall was "as stark a symbol as anyone could ever expect to see of the contrast between two different political systems: on one side, people held captive by a failed and corrupt totalitarian government, on the other, freedom, enterprise, prosperity."[26]

Two months before the president's address in Berlin, Peter Robinson, Reagan's gifted wordsmith, had been assigned to write the speech. His task was to somehow harness the passion behind Reagan's long-standing war against Communism and channel it into words that could spark a silent coup—one powerful enough to push down a wall. That, after all, had been Reagan's goal all along, even before becoming president. But no one, least of whom Robinson, had any idea that the speech would become the historic oration that it did.

Several world leaders had recently participated in the celebrations surrounding the 750th anniversary of the founding of Berlin when Robinson and the White House advance team, Secret Service agents, and press officials visited the city to prepare for the presidential visit. Robinson decided that the best way to gather material for the speech was to mill among the people and listen. He says one experience, more than any other, had been the genesis for the speech's most famous line:

> That evening, I broke away from the advance team to join a dozen Berliners for dinner. Our hosts were Dieter and Ingeborg Elz.... Although we had never met, we had friends in common, and the Elzes had offered to put on the dinner party to give me a feel for

their city. . . . "Have you gotten used to the wall?" The Elzes and their guests glanced at each other uneasily. . . . Then one man raised an arm and pointed. "My sister lives twenty miles in that direction," he said. "I haven't seen her in more than two decades. Do you think I can get used to that?" . . . Our hostess broke in. A gracious woman, she had suddenly grown angry. Her face was red. She made a fist with one hand and pounded it into the palm of the other. "If this man Gorbachev is serious with his talk of *glasnost* and *perestroika,*" she said, "he can prove it. He can get rid of this wall."[27]

Presidential speechwriters often bemoan how the White House briefing protocol for major White House speeches often eviscerates the best parts of a speech, and Reagan's Berlin address proved no different. A debate among those inside the president's inner circle had erupted over complaints from some in the State Department and National Security Council (NSC), who felt that certain passages in the president's speech would be ill received by the Soviets and were too strident and undiplomatic in tone. When Dick Wirthlin discussed the hand-wringing among some of the diplomats, Reagan told him, "I want it to stay in, Dick. It's what I want to say."

Wirthlin replied, "Mr. President, I agree with you. But you know the diplomats are going to give us trouble on this one."

"Let them. I want it in," said Reagan.[28]

Just before he was to speak at the Brandenburg Gate, President Reagan's West German hosts had taken him to a government building near the Berlin Wall. He was warned that just across the wall on the eastern side was a building where the Communists housed a long-distance monitoring device that could eavesdrop on conversations. "Watch what you say," one German official warned Reagan. "Well, when I heard that," said Reagan, "I went out to a landing that was even closer to the building and began sounding off about what I thought [of] a government that penned in its people like farm animals. I can't remember exactly what I said, but I may have used a little profanity in expressing my opinion of Communism, hoping I would be heard."[29]

Reagan was then taken to the Brandenburg Gate, where tens of thousands of Berliners, many waving U.S. and German flags, had assembled. The speaking platform had been constructed against the Berlin Wall, with the Brandenburg Gate soaring above and behind it. A baby blue backdrop with a Plexiglass bulletproof window provided presidential protection, but it also allowed the Berlin Wall to remain in view.[30] Flanking both sides of the window were alternating German and U.S. flags. Wrapping the dais was a thick banner in the colors of the German flag: red, gold, and black.

Reagan, now seventy-six years old, stepped out onto the dais and took to the lectern:

> *Twenty-four years ago, President John F. Kennedy visited Berlin, and speaking to the people of this city and the world at the city hall. Well, since then two other presidents have come, each in his turn to Berlin. And today, I, myself, make my second visit to your city. . . .*
>
> *Our gathering today is being broadcast throughout Western Europe and North America. I understand that it is being seen and heard as well in the East. To those listening throughout Eastern Europe, I extend my warmest greetings and the good will of the American people. To those listening in East Berlin, a special word: Although I cannot be with you, I address my remarks to you just as surely as to those standing here before me. For I join you, as I join your fellow countrymen in the West, in this firm, this unalterable belief:* Es gibt nur ein Berlin. *[There is only one Berlin].*

Reagan's reference to President Kennedy's speech in Berlin had been somewhat obligatory. Kennedy had famously said, "*Ich bin ein Berliner!*" But there was another, more serious reason why it made sense to reference President Kennedy: the Berlin Wall had been constructed in the early hours of August 13, 1961, on Kennedy's watch. As Schweizer records:

> West Berlin residents awoke to see that a massive wall had been erected through their city. Within a matter of hours, they had been encircled by concrete and barbed wired. Suddenly, friends and family were divided. Kennedy was furious at the action, but he was not prepared to go very far in countering it. . . . "It seems particularly stupid," [Kennedy] told aides, "to risk killing a million Americans over an argument about access rights on the Autobahn.

Nikita Krushchev told Robert Frost that Kennedy was "too liberal to fight."[31] By contrast, Reagan had the Republican tradition of using military strength to deter aggression filling his sails and propelling him forward. He believed in achieving peace through strength.

> *Behind me stands a wall that encircles the free sectors of this city, part of a vast system of barriers that divides the entire continent of Europe. From the Baltic South, those barriers cut across Germany in a gash of barbed wire, concrete, dog runs, and guard towers. Farther south, there may be no visible, no obvious wall. But there remain armed guards and checkpoints all the same—still a restriction on the right to travel, still an instrument to impose upon ordinary men and women the will of a totalitarian state.*
>
> *Yet, it is here in Berlin where the wall emerges most clearly; here, cutting across your city, where the news photo and the television screen have imprinted this brutal division of a continent upon the mind of the world. Standing before the Brandenburg Gate, every man is a German separated from his fellow men. Every man is a Berliner, forced to look upon a scar. . . .*
>
> *Yet, I do not come here to lament. For I find in Berlin a message of hope, even in the shadow of this wall, a message of triumph. . . .*

In the Communist world, we see failure, technological back-wardness, declining standards of health, even want of the most basic kind—too little food. Even today, the Soviet Union still cannot feed itself. After these four decades, then, there stands before the entire world one great and inescapable conclusion: Freedom leads to prosperity. Freedom replaces the ancient hatreds among the nations with comity and peace. Freedom is the victor.

Applause and cheers from his West German crowd punctuated many of Reagan's lines. His audience knew the truth of his words. They had lived them. Just as the Elzes had told Peter Robinson over dinner, families had been split in two and separated for decades. But Reagan's words weren't just intended for those in the West. He had been informed that some in the Communist East were picking up his speech through radio frequencies. Just as Natan Sharansky, the Jewish refusenik, had been heartened in the gulags when he heard Reagan condemn the Soviet Union as an "evil empire," so, too, had Reagan hoped his words would provide solace for those listening in fear of the totalitarian regime that enslaved them.

Reagan's use of light and dark imagery and of surgical or medical metaphors was striking. Twice in his address Reagan refers to the Berlin Wall as a scar, and twice he says this gash cut through the city. In this way, he transformed the wall into a wound, a glaring blight on an otherwise great and proud 750-year-old city. It had all been part of Reagan's strategy to heap international pressure, shame, and embarrassment on the Soviet Union. As one NSC staffer put it, the Soviets needed "to be reminded that the wall is a public relations disaster."[32] Reagan sought to magnify the festering wound for all the world to see. So he pressed on: "In the Communist world, we see failure, technological backwardness, declining standards of health, even want of the most basic kind—too little food."

The Berliners' cheers and the sight of U.S. and German flags waving in celebration generated devastating images for the Soviets, even as Communism's "slaves," as Lady Margaret Thatcher once called them, were literally on the other side of the wall. Reagan continued:

> *We welcome change and openness; for we believe that freedom and security go together, that the advance of human liberty—the advance of human liberty can only strengthen the cause of world peace.*
>
> *There is one sign the Soviets can make that would be unmistakable, that would advance dramatically the cause of freedom and peace.*
>
> *General Secretary Gorbachev, if you seek peace, if you seek prosperity for the Soviet Union and Eastern Europe, if you seek liberalization: Come here to this gate.*
>
> *Mr. Gorbachev, open this gate.*

The audience sent forth a burst of "hoorays" and applause.

> *Mr. Gorbachev—Mr. Gorbachev, tear down this wall!*

A thunderous, guttural roar erupted from the German audience. Here was an American president saying what they had been so afraid to say themselves, the very thing their family members imprisoned on the other side of the wall could *not* say.

> *East and West do not mistrust each other because we are armed; we are armed because we mistrust each other. And our differences are not about weapons but about liberty. When President Kennedy spoke at the City Hall those 24 years ago, freedom was encircled; Berlin was under siege. And today, despite all the pressures upon this city, Berlin stands secure in its liberty. And freedom itself is transforming the globe. . . .*
>
> *Yet in this age of redoubled economic growth, of information and innovation, the Soviet Union faces a choice: It must make fundamental changes, or it will become obsolete. . . .*

> *And I invite Mr. Gorbachev: Let us work to bring the East-
> ern and Western parts of the city closer together, so that all the
> inhabitants of all Berlin can enjoy the benefits that come with
> life in one of the great cities of the world. . . .*
>
> *The totalitarian world produces backwardness because it does
> such violence to the spirit, thwarting the human impulse to cre-
> ate, to enjoy, to worship.*

This passage is another example of Reagan's rhetorical deftness; he landed a clenched fist wrapped in a velvet glove. In one portion, Reagan is poking and jabbing at the Soviet scar, lamenting Communism's lagging economic performance, stressing the Soviet system's inability to keep up technologically—yet another example of Communism's "backward" nature (the second time he uses the term)—presaging the demise of the Soviet Union, and declaring it "backward" (for the second time, no less). But just a few sentences later, Reagan extends an olive branch and urges mutual cooperation. This style of punching and hugging, of rhetorical bobbing and weaving, was a hallmark of the Reagan style.

> *The totalitarian world finds even symbols of love and of wor-
> ship an affront. Years ago, before the East Germans began
> rebuilding their churches, they erected a secular structure: the tel-
> evision tower at Alexander Platz. Virtually ever since, the
> authorities have been working to correct what they view as the
> tower's one major flaw: treating the glass sphere at the top with
> paints and chemicals of every kind. Yet even today when the sun
> strikes that sphere, that sphere that towers over all Berlin, the
> light makes the sign of the cross. There in Berlin, like the city
> itself, symbols of love, symbols of worship, cannot be suppressed.*

As political scientist Paul Kengor wrote, "Reagan perceived few things as more courageous than standing for God under persecution—particularly communist persecution."[33] Rhetoric scholars, such as Kurt Ritter and David Henry, have identified Reagan's myriad uses of religious imagery and themes throughout his rhetoric.[34] When Reagan uttered the phrase "sign of the cross," his audience applauded in a way an American audience never could. Berliners knew of the religious persecution their family and friends on the other side of the wall experienced daily. The idea that, despite the Soviets' fiercest efforts, the sign of the cross was irrepressible touched them. Reagan's illustration was about much more than refracted light and its resulting cross-shaped shadow. No, as Reagan and his audience understood, "Like the city itself," this was a small moment with a big meaning; it was further evidence that the "symbols of love, symbols of worship, cannot be suppressed."

> As I looked out a moment ago from the Reichstag, that embodiment of German unity, I noticed words crudely spray-painted upon the wall, perhaps by a young Berliner (quote): "This wall will fall. Beliefs become reality."
>
> Yes, across Europe, this wall will fall, for it cannot withstand faith; it cannot withstand truth. The wall cannot withstand freedom.
>
> And I would like, before I close, to say one word. I have read, and I have been questioned since I've been here about certain demonstrations against my coming. And I would like to say just one thing, and to those who demonstrate so. I wonder if they have ever asked themselves that if they should have the kind of government they apparently seek, no one would ever be able to do what they're doing again. Thank you and God bless you all. Thank you.

When Reagan delivered his line about Communist protests and demonstrations, the audience had responded with almost the same level of jubilance as it had following the utterance of the line for which the speech is named. Reagan couldn't call his critics unthinking and stupid, but it was the next best thing. Democracy, he argued,

was self-reflexive. It can critique itself only because of its own existence. That these truths had been lost on those who espoused social-
ist or Communist doctrines represented yet another "fatal conceit,"
as legendary economic theorist F. A. Hayek once famously wrote.[35]
Gauging from their loud and grateful applause, it was a fact not lost
on the Berliners in Reagan's audience.

On November 9, 1989, the Iron Curtain that had separated East from
West fell. Ronald Reagan had been stubborn, tough, and right. He
had won the Cold War. "I never dreamed that in less than three years
the wall would come down and a six-thousand pound section of it
would be sent to me for my presidential library," said Reagan. But
even if he hadn't dreamed that the wall would come down as fast as
it did, he had dreamed that it would come down. In November 1978,
Reagan stood in front of the Berlin Wall and told his aides, "We have
got to find a way to knock this thing down." Exactly twelve years
later, that is exactly what he did.

——— *10* ———

Newt Gingrich

The Revolutionary Speaker

"The Contract with America"

JANUARY 4, 1995

INAUGURAL SPEECH AS SPEAKER OF THE HOUSE, U.S. HOUSE
OF REPRESENTATIVES, WASHINGTON, D.C.

———————

*We must replace the welfare state with an opportunity
society . . . How can we not decide that this is a moral crisis
equal to segregation, equal to slavery?*

—Newt Gingrich

Newt Gingrich will go down in Republican Party history as one of
the most consequential congressmen ever. As brash as he is brilliant,
as staunch as he was successful, Gingrich engineered the biggest congressional sea change in generations. Democrats had controlled the
U. S. House of Representatives for forty years. In 1994, however, Gingrich, the one-time "backbencher" from Cobb County, Georgia, who
had taken down Democratic Speaker of the House Jim Wright of
Texas, pulled off what few thought possible: a Republican takeover of
the House of Representatives.

Gingrich's Republican landslide did not happen without warning.
In the early 1980s, Gingrich, a member who had once called Speaker
Tip O'Neill a "thug" and Republican senator Bob Dole the "tax col-
lector for the welfare state," had predicted the GOP would take control of the Congress by 1992.[1] His prediction was off by only two
years. But even if he had guessed correctly, the prediction would have
still seemed unthinkable.

Equally surprising was Gingrich's rise to power. Born in 1943, Gingrich had endured a turbulent childhood. After being abandoned by his biological father, he was adopted by parents who had themselves been adopted. Bob Gingrich, Newt's adoptive father, was a stern and distant man. The two fought endlessly. In a 1995 interview with *Vanity Fair*, Bob Gingrich, a former colonel in the army, said that "some people thought I was too rough with Newt. I just wanted him to get out of the house and earn a living." He then confessed that he never hugged Newt. "You don't do that with boys. I didn't even do it with my girls." He then explained that saying "I love you" was unnecessary; according to his philosophy: "If I tell you once, that's all that's necessary. If it ever changes, I'll let you know."[2]

As a boy, Gingrich fell in love with history. His father's military assignment landed the family in France and later in Germany, and these experiences affected young Newt deeply. Touring famous World War I and II battlefields fueled in him a passion for all things historical. In 1971 he was awarded a doctorate in history from Tulane University. As a history professor teaching at West Georgia College, Gingrich made two failed attempts to win a seat in Congress. His third run in 1978, however, proved victorious. His hard-driving style quickly swayed many conservative Republican members and resulted in his takedown of Democratic Speaker of the House Jim Wright. Having proved himself a fierce partisan, Gingrich set out to take back the House of Representatives.

During a January 1994 House Republican conference weekend retreat in Salisbury, Maryland, Gingrich and several others met to develop a master strategy for the November midterm elections. Republican pollster Frank Luntz was one of those present. Gingrich believed the GOP could "nationalize" the election by crafting a legislative blueprint to which all Republican candidates could pledge allegiance. For such an approach to work, the components of this contract would need to garner strong public support, regardless of region or partisanship. Luntz then identified so-called 60 percent issues—policy positions that were consistently supported by 60 percent or more of voters—that were in keeping with Republican values and principles. From these issues, ten policy initiatives and positions were chosen. According to Gingrich, Americans backed the majority of these items by 80 percent or more. Even the least popular issue, regulatory reform and litigation reform, still had 60 percent support.[3] This ten-point policy agenda became known as the Contract with America.

Through a rigorous process of candidate recruitment and training, future Speaker Gingrich had assembled his Republican regiments and whipped them into top electoral form. On a windy September 27 afternoon, just two months before the midterm election, Gingrich and his recruits stood on the steps of the Capitol to declare a unified front that supported the Contract with America and opposed congressional Democrats. "The Washington press corps immediately got it into their heads that the Contract was a big mistake," said Gingrich. "Reporter after reporter, columnist after columnist, declared that we had blown our chances just as it appeared we might win a majority." But Gingrich and the Republicans had done their homework. They knew voters were overwhelmingly with them on the issues. Having reporters and Democrats align against their popular policies would only calcify Republicans' belief that the media were liberal and out of touch with voters. "For our part," said Gingrich, "the Contract brought our campaign completely into focus. The sense that victory was within our grasp made a big difference in the campaign. . . . It is harder to raise money when major donors know the Democrats are going to win. By October most of our people were convinced we could win. It gave us a heady boost in morale and resources."[4]

Meanwhile, leading up to the 1994 election, many conservative voices had been calling for a conservative revival. Having lost to Bill Clinton in 1992, Republicans were reeling. The fact that Clinton had been elected a minority president with only 43 percent of the popular vote only added to the sting. Indeed, had Ross Perot not siphoned off 19 percent of the popular vote, many believed Republicans would have maintained control of the White House. George H. W. Bush's mistake, they believed, was that he had betrayed the conservative philosophy of smaller government and lower taxes espoused by Ronald Reagan. This sentiment could even be seen in the titles of some conservative books published before the 1994 election. Chief among them was a book written by a young conservative, David Frum, who would later become a speechwriter for George W. Bush. The book's title, *Dead Right*, was especially gloomy. The cover even contained an ominous if constructive warning: "The great conservative revival of the 1980s is over. Government is bigger, taxes are higher, family values are weaker, and the Democrats are in power. What will the Right do next?"[5]

It was a question Gingrich had already answered. In November 1994, Republican congressional candidates ousted fifty-two Democrats, including Democratic Speaker of the House Tom Foley. For the first time in forty years, Republicans regained the majority in the U.S. House of Representatives. The Washington, D.C., establishment was stunned. The Contract with America whipped the GOP message into a united and singular voice that resonated with voters who were fed up with what they perceived as an inefficient and bloated government. Using a message of personal responsibility and governmental efficiency, Gingrich had masterminded the most sweeping electoral victory in a generation. Republicans now had a majority and a mandate. They also had a revolutionary leader whose words spoken during his inaugural address would reconfigure the legislative terrain.

On January 4, 1995, Dick Gephardt handed Gingrich the Speaker's gavel and with it the shape of government to come. After thanking a bipartisan cast of individuals, the soon to be sworn in Speaker of the House began doing precisely what his Contract with America promised—change the direction and size of the federal government:

> *We are starting the 104th Congress . . . this will be the busiest day on opening day in congressional history. I want to read just a part of the Contract with America. I don't mean this as a partisan act, but rather to remind all of us what we are about to go*

through and why. Those of us who ended up in the majority stood on these steps and signed a contract, and here is part of what it says: On the first day of the 104th Congress the new Republican majority will immediately pass the following reforms aimed at restoring the faith and trust of the American people in their government: First, require all laws that apply to the rest of the country also to apply equally to the Congress. Second, select a major, independent auditing firm to conduct a comprehensive audit of the Congress for waste, fraud or abuse. Third, cut the number of House committees and cut committee staffs by a third. Fourth, limit the terms of all committee chairs. Fifth, ban the casting of proxy votes in committees. Sixth, require committee meetings to be open to the public. Seven, require a three-fifths majority vote to pass a tax increase. Eight, guarantee an honest accounting of our federal budget by implementing zero baseline budgeting. . . . We then say that within the first 100 days of the 104th Congress we shall bring to the House floor the following bills, each to be given full and open debate, each to be given a full and clear vote, and each to be immediately available for inspection. We made it available that day. We listed ten items. A balanced budget amendment and line-item veto, a bill to stop violent criminals, emphasizing among other things an effective and enforceable death penalty. Third was welfare reform. Fourth, legislation protecting our kids. Fifth was to provide tax cuts for families. Sixth was a bill to strengthen our national defense. Seventh was a bill to raise the senior citizens' earning limit. Eighth was legislation rolling back Government regulations. Ninth was a commonsense legal reform bill, and tenth was congressional term limits legislation.

It was an ambitious agenda. But like a floodgate with a rising and roiling tide behind it, Speaker Gingrich knew that once he had unlatched the 1994 electoral gate, his poll-tested policy initiatives had the political momentum necessary to race forward. The Contract with America had homed in on voters' desire for a legislative agenda grounded in the kind of conservative philosophy found in books like Marvin Olasky's *The Tragedy of American Compassion*, Charles Murray's *Losing Ground*, and Myron Magnet's *The Dream and the Nightmare*, books Gingrich often cited as having been pivotal in winning "the argument about the need to replace a destructive system of dependency with a system of effort and opportunity."[6]

The Contract with America was focused on achieving results— and quickly. Almost a decade later, Gingrich said the reason the Contract was effective was because it wasn't merely a political campaign ploy, but instead an actionable blueprint for governmental change. By labeling it a "contract," Republicans had co-opted the language of the marketplace and moved beyond empty promises. What made the document different was that it had teeth; it demanded from its signatories that they would produce up or down votes on all ten items. As the final line of the Contract declared, "If we break this promise, throw us out."[7]

While fiscal responsibility and free enterprise lay at the heart of much of the Contract, Gingrich wanted to rebuild the bridge between entrepreneurialism and the positive moral virtues it could produce, such as hard work, creativity, discipline, and the means to help others. As Speaker Gingrich later wrote in his book *To Renew America*, "Generosity, trust, optimism, and hard work—these are the elements that have driven the American entrepreneurial system, creating the most powerful and vibrant economy the world has ever known. . . . The welfare system has sapped the spirit of the poor and made it harder to climb the first rungs of the economic ladder."[8] Despite his critics' characterizations of him as being a brusque, insensitive, "right-wing Republican," those who had actually listened to his inaugural address heard the voice of someone who longed to see individuals achieve their full potential:

> *Beyond the Contract I think there are two giant challenges. . . .*
> *Let me talk very briefly about both challenges. First, on the bal-*

anced budget. . . . We must replace the welfare state with an opportunity society. The balanced budget is the right thing to do. But it does not in my mind have the moral urgency of coming to grips with what is happening to the poorest Americans. . . . I do not believe that there is a single American who can see a news report of a 4-year-old thrown off of a public housing project in Chicago by other children and killed and not feel that a part of your heart went, too. I think of my nephew in the back, Kevin, and how all of us feel about our children. How can any American read about an 11-year-old buried with his Teddy bear because he killed a 14-year-old, and then another 14-year-old killed him, and not have some sense of "My God, where has this country gone?" How can we not decide that this is a moral crisis equal to segregation, equal to slavery? How can we not insist that every day we take steps to do something?

The Contract with America's critique of the welfare state had been devastating. Gingrich had transformed the welfare issue from a purely financial argument into something deeper. He had turned it into a debate over America's moral values. As the previous passage illustrates, and as the books Gingrich will later cite suggest, the Speaker believed that terminal welfare drained individuals' desire to create, to strive, and to achieve. He and his Republican regiments believed that the more government gave a person, the more it could take from him. Lyndon Baines Johnson's so-called Great Society had turned out to be not so great. In truth, a generation of welfare recipients had been raised to accept mediocrity and government dependency as the best one could do. Gingrich argued that segments of the American family had been relegated to a life of hopelessness marked by personal tragedy and despair, emotions not far removed from his own childhood.

I have seldom been more shaken than I was after the election when I had breakfast with two members of the Black Caucus.

One of them said to me, "Can you imagine what it is like to visit a first-grade class and realize that every fourth or fifth young boy in that class may be dead or in jail within 15 years? And they are your constituents and you are helpless to change it?" For some reason, I do not know why, maybe because I visit a lot of schools, that got through. I mean, that personalized it. That made it real, not just statistics, but real people. Then I tried to explain part of my thoughts by talking about the need for alternatives to the bureaucracy, and we got into what I think frankly has been a pretty distorted and cheap debate over orphanages. Let me say, first of all, my father, who is here today, was a foster child. He was adopted as a teenager. I am adopted. We have relatives who were adopted. We are not talking out of some vague impersonal Dickens "Bleak House" middle-class intellectual model. We have lived the alternatives.

Many Americans, including Republicans, were unfamiliar with Gingrich's personal life story. His testimonial in the previous passage revealed the genesis of his ideology. It was also meant to buffer him from attacks. The "rich, white country club" epithets often hurled at the GOP did not apply in Gingrich's, or many others', case. But even before he became Speaker of the House, Gingrich had been no stranger to character assassination, especially on the issue of race. "The Georgia I entered was bitterly segregationist," Gingrich remembers. "It always amuses me when reporters and columnists assume I must be a traditional southern conservative with, they hint, racist and redneck roots. . . . Segregation had been erected by the southern Democratic Party to give power to white elites by splitting poor people of both races."[9]

It is also worth noting that one of Gingrich's most common rhetorical "moves" involves the dropping of books and authors into his speeches, as if to leave an "intellectual bread crumb trail" for the listener to follow. Gingrich mentions the titles of four books and explicitly recommends that listeners read Marvin Olasky's *The Tragedy of American Compassion.* His mention of Dickens's *Bleak House* served to distance himself from critics who argued that he was intent on returning the United States to a draconian past. Exactly the reverse, Gingrich argued. The new Speaker wanted to redefine compassion. Governmental largesse cast to the underclass was not only an ineffective way of reducing poverty, he argued. It was the *opposite* of compassion; it was cruelty. Given his experience as an abandoned child who was later adopted, the new Speaker's last line had packed an ethos-laden punch: "We have lived the alternatives."

I believe when we are told that children are so lost in the city bureaucracies that there are children who end up in dumpsters, when we are told that there are children doomed to go to schools where seventy or eighty percent of them will not graduate, when we are told of public housing projects that are so dangerous that if any private sector ran them they would be put in jail, and the only solution we are given is, "Well, we will study it, we will get around to it," my only point is that this is unacceptable. We can find ways immediately to do things better, to reach out, break through the bureaucracy and give every young American child a better chance. . . . If you cannot afford to leave the public housing project, you are not free. If you do not know how to find a job and do not know how to create a job, you are not free. If you cannot find a place that will educate you, you are not free. If you are afraid to walk to the store because you could get killed, you are not free. . . . I want to close by reminding all of us of how much bigger this is than us. . . . All I can do is pledge to you that, if each of us will reach out prayerfully and try to genuinely understand each other, if we will recognize that in this building we symbolize America, and that we have an obligation to talk with each other, then I think a year from now we can look on the 104th Congress as a truly amazing institution without regard to party, without regard to ideology. We can say, "Here

America comes to work, and here we are preparing for those chil-dren a better future." Thank you. Good luck and God bless you.

Through his antistrophe refrain "you are not free," the history pro-fessor turned Speaker ushered in the Republican revolution. The Contract with America had provided the new GOP majority with clear and popular marching orders, and those marching orders had at their root a moral mission: roll back the failed policies of the New Deal and Great Society by reinvigorating a spirit of opportunity and competitive drive by reducing the federal regulations and intrusions that squelch human flourishing.[10] Republicans kept their word. In the first ninety-three days of their tenure, the 104th Congress voted on all ten of the initiatives contained in the Contract with America. As Gingrich wrote in his 2005 version of the Contract with America, the original Contract accomplished:

1. The first major tax cut in sixteen years.

2. Real welfare reform, reducing the number of people on wel-fare by 60 percent and insisting that welfare recipients go to school or look for a job.

3. The first four consecutive balanced budgets since the 1920s, enabling our economy to enter a long period of very low interest rates with little risk of inflation.

4. The first financial audit of the House by an outside auditing firm in U.S. history, a practice that continues today.

5. Term limits for committee chairs in the House.

6. Applying to the House all the laws that apply to small busi-nesses so politicians can learn what the self-employed and small business men and women endure from government.

7. Strengthening the military and intelligence capabilities of the United States.

8. The invention of the Thomas system, which allows Internet access to the U.S. House of Representatives, bypassing lobby-ists and privileged insiders.[11]

Beyond its impressive legislative achievements, the 1994 Republican takeover increased the GOP vote by nine million from the 1990 election and produced a one-million vote decline among Democrats. "This swing of ten million votes between the two parties," wrote Gingrich, "is the largest non-presidential voter shift in American history. It had an impact on Senate elections, governorships, state legislative races, and every level of American politics."[12]

Gingrich's standing as the leading Republican "idea man" and master strategist, combined with his blunt, confrontational style, soon made him a target. Just one year after his inaugural speech, two *Washington Post* reporters (one of whom became Clinton's biographer) had already written the book *"Tell Newt to Shut Up!"* a quote that the authors said belonged to many of Gingrich's closest allies by year's end.[13] Indeed, following the disappointing 1998 midterm congressional elections, Republicans had *lost* seats despite the fact that a Democratic president occupied the White House. This, combined with Gingrich's polarizing public persona, encouraged the revolutionary Republican leader to resign both his position as Speaker as well as his seat in Congress.

Today, even self-described liberal members of the media like *Time* magazine columnist Joe Klein concede that "[t]here was always another side to Newt. He was an intellectually honest policy wonk with an appetite for taking on the most important issues facing society—poverty, education, health care, national security, the environment," even if his policy prescriptions "were inevitably market-based and conservative."[14] Whether reconsidered appraisals of the Gingrich legacy will result in a future presidential bid remains to be seen. Regardless, one thing is certain: Gingrich's fertile and frenetic mind, as well as his orchestration of the 1994 Republican takeover, will ensure that he remains an influential force in Republican Party politics for years to come.

——11——

George W. Bush

His Mission and His Moment

"Justice Will Be Done"

SEPTEMBER 20, 2001

JOINT SESSION OF CONGRESS, U.S. CAPITOL, WASHINGTON, D.C.

We will not tire, we will not falter, and we will not fail.

—President George W. Bush

On September 11, 2001, at exactly 9:03 a.m., the nose cone of United Airlines Flight 175 punched into the South Tower of the World Trade Center at over 500 miles per hour. The events that unfolded thereafter are both well recorded and excruciating to remember: the planes slamming into the towers; the fireball and shattered glass; the dust-caked faces wandering amid the rumble; the wall of smoke that resembled a tidal wave chasing the terrified survivors as they ran; the firefighters—the heroes—swimming against the human current; people teetering on window ledges, forced into that Godforsaken decision; the final good-byes left on voice mail; and more soot covered heroes.

Almost as if by legal decree, many of these images have since vanished from U.S. televisions and newspapers. But so have the other images, the more hopeful ones: total strangers, arms wrapped tightly around one another; Jews, Christians, and Muslims praying side by side; "God Bless America," the nation's soundtrack; cars, stores, and streets smothered in flags; candlelight vigils and prayer services seemingly around the clock; unity; solidarity; pride—and that speech.

President George W. Bush's September 20, 2001, speech set a young century on its future course. Even those Americans who have now since returned to their September 10 levels of animosity toward President Bush can recall snippets of that speech. For many, it will forever be the "We will not tire, we will not falter, and we will not fail" speech. For others, it remains the "Our mission and our moment" speech. And for still others, Bush's address will go down as the "Whether we bring our enemies to justice, or bring justice to our enemies, justice will be done" speech. Regardless of what Americans choose to call it, one thing is certain: Bush's September 20 address to a joint session of Congress will remain his finest and most famous address.

David Zarefsky, a presidential rhetoric scholar and Northwestern University professor of speech communication, wrote, "On September 20, 2001, President George W. Bush rose to the occasion. He and his writers found the right words, the right themes, the right voice."[1] Indeed, the temporal context, the speech's magisterial craftsmanship, the foreign policy stratagems embedded in it, and its large and listening audience coalesced to create a history-making speech.

But it was more than that. With "Clash of Civilizations" rhetoric buzzing across the country, it was the unmistakably religious-laden themes and language of Bush's speech that gave it its American resonance and Republican velocity. One has to go back to Ronald Reagan's "evil empire" speech to find another presidential pronouncement quite like it. All U.S. presidents have at times invoked the Almighty in their speeches. But as Reagan speechwriter Peggy Noonan wrote in her *Wall Street Journal* column the week following Bush's address, "It seemed to me a God-touched moment and a God-touched speech.... He talked of prayer like a man who'd been praying, and who understood that tens of millions of Americans and others throughout the world were his powerful prayer warriors. They prayed the right thing would be said and done. It was."[2] As the behind-the-scenes story of Bush's September 20 speech reveals,

Bush's address was not just a defining foreign policy declaration. Bush's words were also intended to be an attack on postmodern relativism that deftly embraced religious tolerance while proudly espousing the virtue of democratic doctrine.

At 9:07 a.m., just minutes after Islamic radicals slammed United Airlines Flight 175 and American Airlines Flight 11 into the south and north towers of the World Trade Center, respectively, Andrew Card, the president's chief of staff, approached the president and whispered in his ear, "A second plane has hit the second tower." Bush was in Sarasota, Florida, that day reading to students at Emma Booker Elementary School as part of his early effort to build support for the No Child Left Behind Act. After delivering a short televised message at 9:30, Bush asked the children to bow their heads for a moment of silence. "They had declared war on us," Bush later told Bob Woodward, "and I made up my mind at that moment that we were going to war."[3]

In the nine days between the terrorist attacks on the Twin Towers, the Pentagon, and Flight 93, Bush made other speeches before his historic address. There was his 217-word blip of a speech delivered from Barksdale Air Force Base followed by an Oval Office address that same evening. Three days later Bush gave a stirring yet tempered address at the Episcopal National Cathedral as part of the National Day of Prayer and Remembrance. But behind the scenes, Bush, a man who begins each day by reading the scriptures, had like most Americans been torn between grief and rage. Shortly after the attack, for example, the president had told Vice President Dick Cheney, "We're going to find out who is responsible for this and we're going to kick their asses."[4] And then, three days before his speech to a joint session of Congress, Bush had upset First Lady Laura Bush when he said to a group of reporters following a Pentagon briefing, "I want justice. And there's an old poster out West . . . I recall, that said, 'Wanted, Dead or Alive.'"

All this was both natural and to be expected, especially for the Texan Bush. Even Bush has at times recognized that his words may seem overly muscular. For example, in an attempt to take the edge off his sometimes sharp public persona in time for reelection, Bush would later poke fun at himself during his 2004 Republican National Convention acceptance speech: "You may have noticed I have a few flaws, too. People sometimes have to correct my English. I knew I had a problem when Arnold Schwarzenegger started doing it. Some folks look at me and see a certain swagger, which in Texas is called 'walking.' Now and then I come across as a little too blunt, and for that we can all thank the white-haired lady [Barbara Bush] sitting right up there."

But it was the balancing of these two sides of Bush—indeed, of America—that would find equilibrium in what was an enormously difficult rhetorical situation. On the one hand, Bush's major televised address had to calm fears, stress tolerance for Muslims, provide solace to the nation's grief, and begin the process of national healing as a sign of U.S. resiliency. On the other hand, the president had to provide a strong vision for how U.S. foreign policy would stop future attacks, rhetorically anticipate the tendency on the left to draw moral equivalency between the attacks of fundamentalist Islamic terrorists and U.S. policies (what conservatives often call the "blame America first" impulse), and carve out in clear and unflinching terms how to prosecute the global war on terrorism. In short, Bush had to bridge the two sides of himself—the devout man of faith and the Texas gunslinger—into a single, coherent historic message.

As veteran *Washington Post* journalists Dan Balz and Bob Woodward wrote, "No presidential speech in recent history would be more important to national morale or more scrutinized than this one."[5] What's more, Bush had only nine short days to prepare. That was still too long for some. Congressional leaders were putting heat on the president to decide whether he would make a speech to a joint session of Congress. One of Bush's quirks is that he never commits to a major speech until he has weighed all his options and seen a final draft of the proposed speech, and this situation was no different. Andy Card, a die-hard Bush loyalist with a soft managerial touch, was busy buying his president some time. Card told members of Congress there was no need to rush. "The president doesn't have to be rushed," Card told them. "He needs to be comfortable with this. We still have time."[6]

Influencing Bush's thoughts and words during this period of preparation were his morning scripture readings, something that would undoubtedly horrify his liberal secular critics. Indeed, the president's much maligned and mocked reference to terrorists as "evildoers" was the product of a morning Bible devotional reading shortly after 9/11.[7] Bush had awoken and read Proverbs 21:15, "When justice is done, it brings joy to the righteous but terror to evildoers."[8]

Meanwhile, the president's chief speechwriter, Michael J. Gerson, "the Scribe," as Bush called him, had yet to begin crafting the language of a possible Bush speech until he had received the green light from Karen Hughes, one of the president's longtime advisers and most trusted strategists. Hughes and Karl Rove, an adviser and chief political strategist for Bush, had met Sunday afternoon in the White House to urge the president to deliver a prime-time speech before Congress. Bush, however, refused to commit to the venue until he'd seen a speech draft. Waiting also had the added benefit of allowing the president's military planners and the National Security Council to begin crafting the military response. Still, Bush told Hughes and Rove he would review any speech draft they had the speechwriters prepare.

Following their meeting, Hughes says she made "a huge mistake" in not calling Gerson that evening to get him and the other speechwriters, Matt Scully and John McConnell, cracking on a first draft. But it was a Sunday, and because Gerson had small children, Hughes didn't want to disturb him. Besides, she thought to herself, Gerson probably wouldn't get started writing that night anyhow. But the next morning when Hughes entered the Oval Office she realized she had miscalculated.

"How's the speech coming?" the president asked her.

"I'm going to get with Mike and go over it this morning," Hughes told the president.

"Good, because I want to see a draft tonight."

"Mr. President, that's just impossible," Hughes protested.

"By seven," Bush said with a smile.

When Hughes called Gerson, the speechwriter had the same

reaction that she had had. But Bush had made his expectations clear, so Gerson, Scully, and McConnell got to work.[9]

Joint collaboration was nothing new for the three presidential speechwriters. In the modern era, most presidential speeches are, in fact, written in "committee"—multiple speechwriters working on different sections of the same speech. The task of weaving the disparate pieces of Bush's speeches together fell to Gerson. Indeed, Gerson and George W. Bush share a special relationship. The two men connected early on, something many in the inner circle attribute to their deep mutual Evangelical Christian faith. "You can count on Mike to ask how a given policy will affect the least among us," says Rove. "The shorthand, political way to say it is that Mike is the one always wondering how we can achieve liberal goals with conservative means."[10]

Gerson and Bush are also a contrast in both appearance and personality. Reporter Carl Cannon describes Gerson as "slightly built, not tall, with Clark Kent glasses and a physical modesty that almost, but not quite, hides an ever-present nervous mental energy." Where Bush radiates confidence and bravado, Gerson is shy and reserved, traits developed in college. Bush spent his days at Yale enjoying the social dimensions of college life and playing sports. Gerson's experience as a student at Wheaton College, a well-known Evangelical Christian college in suburban Chicago, had produced a deep theological thinker and a lover of poetry and classical literature with little interest or use for the trivialities of sports. These differences are also reflected in each man's temperament and working style. Former Bush speechwriter David Frum describes the contrast well:

> Bush admired Gerson's deep and animating religious faith. While Bush's Christianity often seemed at odds with his sharp and competitive character, Gerson's grew naturally out of his amiable personality. . . . [Gerson] was as anxious as Bush was confident. When a major speech came due, you would often see Gerson wandering through the presidential complex, squinting at a pad of paper covered with his wild, illegible scrawl, mumbling to himself, and

making orator's gestures with his free hand as he walked. Rove once showed one of Gerson's pads to a reporter and said: "You know, when these go into the archives, future generations will be amazed that we let a crazy person this close to the president of the United States."[11]

Gerson's anxious nature also created certain writing rituals and behaviors. For example, he often preferred to write at the Starbucks near the White House and had also taken on the habit of nervously gnawing the ends of his black pens to the point of exploding. "He ate his way through about a box a week," says Frum. "I once suggested to him that a diet of pencils might be healthier, or anyway less messy, but the habits of a lifetime are hard to break."[12] Gerson's internalized pressure and stress, however, produced serious, life-threatening consequences: "I'm a worrier. I put a lot of pressure on myself. I know people think it's funny, but these aren't charming eccentricities. When I had my heart attack, my doctor was very clear that I had to find a different way to work."[13]

But Gerson's brush with mortality came five years after Bush's historic speech. And at the time, Bush was hardly concerned about putting too much pressure on his speechwriters. The president had made it clear: he wanted the first draft of the speech by seven o'clock. Gerson, Scully, and McConnell came close; they turned in the first draft by eight. Hughes felt the first draft was impressive, especially given the incredibly short amount of time the speechwriters had been given. But Bush is an exacting editor; he still had major problems with portions of the speech. If the president were to agree to give a national address on Thursday, the White House team would have to notify the press by Wednesday, only two days away. Early Wednesday afternoon, Hughes and Bush met in the Oval Office. "Mr. President," said Hughes, "we think we have a great speech now." "Let's tell the Congress," the president said. The speech was scheduled.[14]

On Thursday, September 20, 2001, just hours before President Bush was to speak before a joint session of Congress and an estimated eighty million Americans watching on television, twenty-seven religious leaders of myriad faiths—Buddhist, Hindu, Sikh, Mormon, Jewish, and Christian—arrived at the White House. They had come at Bush's request and were soon ushered into the Roosevelt Room before taking their seats in a circle of chairs. The president sat and joined the men of faith. "I need your help as spiritual leaders to be truthful with the American people without creating panic," Bush told them. "Government will do some things, but you need to be praying and be prepared for questions. I was a sinner in need of redemption and I found it. I think this is part of a spiritual awakening in America," said the president.[15]

For non-Evangelical Christians, Bush's candor and bold expressions of faith could be seen as overly rigid or inappropriate. Even when his biblical allusions were more subtle or muted, the president's detractors would often claim that he was using "coded language" to fly under nonbelievers' radar screens and connect with Evangelical Christians. "They're not code words," Gerson told the *Washington Post*, "they're our culture. . . . Just because some people don't get it doesn't mean it's a plot or a secret."[16] Regardless, the president's communication team sometimes got a chuckle at how religiously tone deaf some in the mainstream media seemed to be. During the 2000 presidential campaign, for example, *New York Times* reporter Frank Bruni had been covering one of Bush's speaking appearances when he wrote, "Mr. Bush also offered an interesting variation on the saying about the pot and the kettle. 'Don't be takin' a speck out of your neighbor's eye,' he told the audience, 'when you got a log in your own.'" With a smile, Gerson noted, "No one at the *Times* seemed to know that these were the words of the Sermon on the Mount."[17]

But few allusions would be lost on the religious leaders surrounding Bush inside the Roosevelt Room. What's more, some matched the president in their expressions of faith and the Almighty's purpose in the moment at hand. "Mr. President. I have just come from the World Trade Center site in lower Manhattan," said Gerald Kieschnick, president of the Lutheran Church–Missouri Synod. "I stood where you stood. I saw what you saw. I smelled what you smelled. You not only have a civil calling but a divine calling. . . . You are not just a civil servant, you are a servant of God called for such a time like this," Kieschnick said. "I accept that responsibility," said Bush.[18]

On September 20, 2001, eighty million Americans huddled around their televisions to find "our mission and our moment." Citizens' interest in the speech had been so intense that in Philadelphia, for example, an exhibition professional hockey game had to be stopped when fans demanded that the arena play Bush's address on the video screens overhead. An avid sports fan, the president quickly understood the significance of that moment: "When I really realized the extent to which America wanted to be led was when they stopped the hockey game in Philadelphia. It was unbelievable. . . . They wanted to hear what the commander in chief, the president of the United States, had to say during this moment."[19]

When Bush entered the House chamber, he was met with boisterous bipartisan applause. Representatives and senators cheered and stretched to extend their hands to shake his hand and cheered in support of the commander in chief. Indeed, the spirit of bipartisanship had been so strong that earlier that day President Bill Clinton's able strategist, Paul Begala, had e-mailed Karen Hughes some suggested lines and passages the president might wish to use. Bush ultimately chose not to integrate Begala's suggestions, but as Hughes put it, "It was a nice gesture; he's a partisan, but he's also an American, and he wanted the president to succeed at this important moment for our country."

During Bush's final practice run-through of the speech, it was unclear whether the weight of the past nine days would prevent him from delivering a strong performance. His delivery during the practice section had been off, and he'd even transposed words in the speech without realizing it.[20] But as he waded through the throng of representatives and senators up toward the well of the chamber wearing a navy blue suit with a U.S. flag pin on his left lapel and his trademark ice blue cravat, Bush's countenance appeared strong, serious, and resolved.

The president greeted Speaker of the House Dennis Hastert and Robert Byrd, the president pro tempore of the Senate. And then he spoke:

> *In the normal course of events, Presidents come to this chamber to report on the state of the Union. Tonight, no such report is needed. It has already been delivered by the American people. We have seen it in the courage of passengers, who rushed terrorists to save others on the ground—passengers like an exceptional man named Todd Beamer. And would you please help me to welcome his wife, Lisa Beamer, here tonight.*

Lisa Beamer, the widow whose husband had rallied Flight 93 passengers to fight the al-Qaeda murderers who had taken over the plane with the intention of slamming it into the White House, rose from her seat. The chamber applauded her for half a minute. The president continued:

> *Tonight we are a country awakened to danger and called to defend freedom. Our grief has turned to anger, and anger to resolution. Whether we bring our enemies to justice, or bring justice to our enemies, justice will be done.*

The last line was a chiasmus, a rhetorical device whose syntax follows an A-B-B-A pattern, as in John F. Kennedy's "Ask not what your country (A) can do for you (B), ask what you (B) can do for your country" (A). But more than a deft rhetorical flourish, the line synopsized the president's thesis: the war on terror will be fought on clear moral grounds. This fight, Bush explained, will not succumb to postmodern moral relativism, a view that holds that all Truth is subjective and therefore cynically dismisses notions of good and evil, thereby effectively razing Western civilization's moral code.

While leftist critics, such as Michael Moore, Harry Belafonte, and the late Susan Sontag, soon suggested that the United States was to blame for the attacks and that its president was a terrorist, Bush had already anticipated the protestations of what Jeanne Kirkpatrick once deemed the "blame America first" crowd, who would seek to draw moral equivalency between U.S. soldiers who enter battlefields to fight killers and terrorists who target and murder civilians: "The terrorists' directive commands them to kill Christians and Jews, to kill all Americans, and make no distinctions among military and civilians, including women and children." Thus, in the wake of 9/11 and the president's speech, some culture critics were sanguine that the postmodern project was in retreat and were predicting the "end of postmodernism and its chokehold on the late 20-Century cultural imagination."[21]

The president then pivoted in his speech to fulfill his role as "educator in chief." By stating and answering four key questions on the hearts and minds of a shocked and grieving nation, Bush spoke to the details of how the war on terror would be waged while striking tones of faith and belief. "Americans have many questions tonight," Bush said. "Americans are asking: Who attacked our country?" The president then introduced into the American lexicon names that would become all too familiar: al-Qaeda, Osama bin Laden, and the Taliban regime. Yet the president was careful—some conservative critics later said too careful—in stating that these terrorists had subverted the true tenets of Islam. Bush's call for religious tolerance and pluralism, even as Ground Zero still smoldered, sought to ease tensions between groups and to condemn possible retaliations against Muslim Americans. The president then spoke directly to Muslims worldwide:

> I also want to speak tonight directly to Muslims throughout the world. We respect your faith. It's practiced freely by many millions of Americans, and by millions more in countries that America counts as friends. Its teachings are good and peaceful, and those who commit evil in the name of Allah blaspheme the name of Allah. The terrorists are traitors to their own faith, trying, in effect, to hijack Islam itself.

Gerson explains that the speech's rhetorical positioning on Islam, as well as on other religious faiths, was meant to be a "principled pluralism" that welcomed all religions but that didn't favor any religions in a sectarian way. (He also points out that Bush is the first president to mention "mosques" and "Islam" in an inaugural address.)[22]

The second question on the minds of many citizens, the president said, was: "Why do they hate us?" The answer Bush offered was clear and direct: because they hate freedom in all its varied forms. Again, Bush was careful to bifurcate between the brand of Islam practiced by terrorists versus that of peaceful Muslims. However, Bush warned, the United States would "not be deceived by their pretenses to piety." In one of the most stirring moments in the speech, the president then strategically linked the terrorist attackers' ethos to that of past tyrants using polysyndeton (multiple conjunctions in succession) to build a rhythmic tone leading into an applause-producing crescendo:

> *We have seen their kind before. They are the heirs of all the murderous ideologies of the 20th century. By sacrificing human life to serve their radical visions—by abandoning every value except the will to power—they follow in the path of fascism, and Nazism, and totalitarianism. And they will follow that path all the way to where it ends: in history's unmarked grave of discarded lies.*

The president's last line lingered in the air for a brief second as congressional members marinated their thoughts on the weight of the president's words before pouring forth thunderous and sustained applause. Bush had placed the September 11 terrorists on the time line of tyrannical history and given Americans a lens through which to view the nation's enemies. There would be no hand-wringing about "understanding" the nation's enemy or studying the root causes of why terrorists enjoy killing Americans or anyone else they deem "infidels." This, Bush understood, was a time for moral clarity: the terrorists were evil, period.

Third, the president said, Americans were asking: "How will we fight and win this war?" President Bush then announced the creation of the Office of Homeland Security, as well as its new director, former Pennsylvania governor Tom Ridge. The position would be cabinet level. This agency, the president explained, would be charged with a broader mission: preempting and foiling terrorist plots. This dimension of Bush's national security vision would later become one of the most controversial aspects of the war's execution, particularly as it pertained to Operation Iraqi Freedom.

The war on terror was to be a massive, sustained, and international effort that would draw on the resources and assistance of many. Prime Minister Tony Blair's presence in the gallery was a visual symbol of solidarity. The president declared that the war was to become a global effort: "This is not, however, just America's fight. And what is at stake is not just America's freedom. This is the world's fight. This is civilization's fight. This is the fight of all who believe in progress and pluralism, tolerance and freedom." The president then called on the support of every nation in the form of police forces, intelligence services, and banking systems around the world. "The civilized world is rallying to America's side."

Finally, the president explained that Americans wanted to know "What is expected of us?" He then asked that Americans care for their families, support the victims, cooperate with the thousands of FBI agents at work on the investigation, maintain patience in the face of adversity and tighter security, participate in the U.S. economy, and continue praying for the victims of terror and their families, for the soldiers, sailors, airmen, and marines who would soon wage war, and for the nation as a whole. "Prayer has comforted us in sorrow, and will help strengthen us for the journey ahead," the president said.

Bush then invoked an anaphora to drive home a central theme. Bush's anaphora was a call to unity that was repeated five times in a span of only 110 words: "We will come together." The parallel repetition was then punctuated with perhaps the greatest visual symbol of national unity, a man who had galvanized New Yorkers and displayed world-class leadership in the face of chaos: New York mayor Rudolph Giuliani. The president had introduced Giuliani alongside Governor George Pataki. But when the House chamber erupted with loud cheers and applause, everyone watching knew who the balance of applause was directed toward.

The appearance of Mayor Giuliani ignited a fireworks display of rhetorical stylistic devices—including alliteration and more anaphora and antithesis—and unmistakably religious-laden language:

> *Great harm has been done to us. We have suffered great loss. And in our grief and anger we have found our mission and our moment. Freedom and fear are at war. The advance of human freedom—the great achievement of our time, and the great hope of every time—now depends on us. Our nation—this genera- tion—will lift a dark threat of violence from our people and our future. We will rally the world to this cause by our efforts, by our courage. We will not tire, we will not falter, and we will not fail.*

The phrase "in our grief and anger we have found our mission and our moment" could have just as easily been written to describe Bush's presidency. Bush's erstwhile bursts of anger about "kicking the asses" of those who perpetrated the attacks and wanting to get them "dead or alive" mirrored the first half of the sentence. But the second half of the sentence—"found our mission and our moment"—might just as easily have replaced the word *our* with *my*. Only nine months into his young presidency, the aftermath of the bitter 2000 Florida bal- lot recount had polarized and fractured the United States. This "Red State versus Blue State" reality had yielded in a national approval rat- ing just above 50 percent, hardly a mandate for strong visionary lead- ership. Yet the 9/11 terrorist attacks had in an instant called Bush to the central task for which his presidential leadership will be remem- bered and judged: the prosecution of the war on terrorism.

Also, the line "[f]reedom and fear are at war" was not only a tightly constructed alliterative antithesis designed to juxtapose democracy (freedom) and tyranny (fear), it also presaged the use of those terms a final time in the last sentences of Bush's speech. The applause-inducing anaphora "[w]e will not tire, we will not falter, and we will not fail" served as the perfect distillation of American resolve, fierce determination, and the gritty tenacity that pervades U.S. military history. Moreover, whereas the opening lines of the passage express "harm," "loss," "grief," and "anger," Bush's anaphora completes the human grief cycle by promoting action marked by victory.

It is my hope that in the months and years ahead, life will return almost to normal. We'll go back to our lives and routines, and that is good. Even grief recedes with time and grace. But our resolve must not pass. Each of us will remember what happened that day, and to whom it happened. We'll remember the moment the news came—where we were and what we were doing. Some will remember an image of a fire, or a story of rescue. Some will carry memories of a face and a voice gone forever.

And I will carry this: It is the police shield of a man named George Howard, who died at the World Trade Center trying to save others. It was given to me by his mom, Arlene, as a proud memorial to her son. This is my reminder of lives that ended, and a task that does not end.

I will not forget this wound to our country or those who inflicted it. I will not yield; I will not rest; I will not relent in waging this struggle for freedom and security for the American people.

The course of this conflict is not known, yet its outcome is certain. Freedom and fear, justice and cruelty, have always been at war, and we know that God is not neutral between them.

Fellow citizens, we'll meet violence with patient justice— assured of the rightness of our cause, and confident of the victories to come. In all that lies before us, may God grant us wisdom, and may He watch over the United States of America.

Thank you.

The late and noted rhetorical critic Kenneth Burke once famously wrote, "Identification is compensatory to division. If men were not apart from one another, there would be no need for the rhetorician to proclaim their unity."[23] What Burke meant was that communicators can and must bridge the gaps that divide them from their audiences by identifying with the emotions and experiences they share in common with their audience. Bush's final passages demonstrate a shared emotional experience with his audience while at the same time personalizing his own sense of grief, loss, and determination. Moreover, with three-quarters of the U.S. population describing itself as Christian or Jewish, Bush was on solid ground in intoning Judeo-Christian themes by using words like *grace, justice,* and *God.*

The visual impact of President Bush holding up a police badge was also loaded with significant symbolic meaning. The idea to integrate the police shield into the president's speech belonged to Hughes. She noticed that the president had been carrying George Howard's badge with him as a way of remembering 9/11 and its victims.[24] By displaying the police shield, Bush the Texan, who just days earlier had stated his desire to get Osama bin Laden "dead or alive," presented himself as a sort of proxy sheriff. His use of first person immediately following his display of the fallen hero's police shield reflected Bush's almost instant understanding that the war on terror would be his legacy.

But all this had been building up to something. The strongest statement of moral certitude in Bush's speech had been saved for its closure: "The course of this conflict is not known, yet its outcome is certain," said Bush. "Freedom and fear, justice and cruelty, have always been at war, and we know that God is not neutral between them." These two lines, perhaps more than any others, would draw criticism from the liberal chattering classes. To them, the line reflected a Manichaean worldview, where Americans wear white hats and the terrorists wear dark hats. But much to his critics' chagrin, that had been precisely Bush and Gerson's intent. Indeed, the speech had been a refutation of moral relativism anchored in classic Judeo-Christian notions of good and evil. Hence, the president's last line boldly declared that Americas could be "assured of the rightness of our cause" and "confident of the victories to come," before asking God's wisdom and hand of protection over the United States of America.

.   .   .

In the wake of President Bush's historic address, CNN political analyst William Schneider declared that the public response to the president's speech had been "astounding." Schneider's polling data revealed that 87 percent of the American people gave Bush's speech high marks and that he enjoyed a 90 percent approval rating. As Schneider recognized, "Bush's religious values figured prominently in his address."[25] The president's speech had so strongly connected with Americans that after his address some citizens headed to their computers to e-mail their commander in chief. The following are three of the thousands of e-mails he received:

Date: 09/21/2001 09:06 PM EDT
From: Keith
To: President George W. Bush
Subject: Re-enlist Wishes

Dear Mr. President,

Your speech tonight was glorious and inspirational. I have proudly served my country for over 21 years in the United States Air Force. I had planned on submitting my retirement paperwork next month; however, will now re-enlist as soon as I can. I'm proud to do so and proud you are my Commander. God bless you and the United States of America.

Keith

Date: 09/21/2001 09:56 PM EDT
From: Fred
To: President George W. Bush
Subject:

Dear Mr. President,

Just heard your speech and wish God almighty could turn the clock back and make me 30 instead of 62. I hope everyone in the world heard your speech and runs for cover if they are a part of terrorism. I know I speak for Vets all over the country when I say "if there is anything I can do for you or my country, just call on me." Thank you Mr. President.

Your servant,
Fred[26]

Date: 09/21/2001 02:32 AM EDT
From: A Michigan Family
To: President George W. Bush
Subject: Children's Questions

Dear Mr. President,

Thank you for your very eloquent speech to the Congress. As my two nine-year-old sons sat with their mother and I listening and watching your speech, my one son asked, "Is all of this because of what happened last week to the people in New York and Washington?" I said, "Yes it is." He said, "Daddy, this must be pretty important, isn't it?" I said, "Yes it is." He said, "Couldn't we just close all of the tunnels and bridges and airports to the rest of the world so that no one could get in?" I answered to him that doing that would not let Americans be free. We would be defeating our selves instead of defeating the terrorists.

He said, "Is the President going to make sure that we will be free?" I said that the President, our neighbors, our soldiers, and our family will make sure that America will always be free.

"Good," he said. "This is important. It's good to be free. We should always be free."

My heart swelled with the pride that a father can only feel for his son, knowing that even at nine years old, a boy in America understands what the terrorists will never know.

God Bless us all.
A Michigan Family
Michigan[27]

Bush's speech had galvanized the American people. It had done so by navigating between the Scylla of tolerance and the Charybdis of moral clarity based on Judeo-Christian notions of good versus evil, right versus wrong. Bush's speech laid out his case for preemptive war, justified a strong military response at the choosing of America's time, created the Office of Homeland Security, memorialized the victims of the terrorist attacks, called for international unity and resolve, and sent a clear message that there were but two sides in the war on terror: "Either you are with us, or you are with the terrorists. From this day forward, any nation that continues to harbor or support terrorism will be regarded by the United States as a hostile regime."

And yet, for all of Bush's success, his critics continued to grouse that his infusion of Judeo-Christian language inched toward the same theocratic style that had created the Taliban, al-Qaeda, and Osama bin Laden. Moreover, some remained extremely uncomfortable by the notion that the Hand of Providence had tapped Bush as the right man for the moment. To them it seemed the height of hubris to believe that God had a plan for each life and that He had appointed Bush to stand in the breach at such a critical moment in time.[28] But these criticisms seemed not to faze Bush. The president knew what he believed, and he knew what the majority of Americans believed.

Following the president's speech, Gerson received a phone call. It was Bush. The president wanted to thank his chief speechwriter for his hard work on the speech. "Mr. President, this is why God wants you here," said Gerson. "No," the president replied "this is why God wants *us* here."[29]

John McCain

The Maverick and His Message

"A Disingenuous Filmmaker"

AUGUST 30, 2004

REPUBLICAN NATIONAL CONVENTION,

MADISON SQUARE GARDEN, NEW YORK, NEW YORK

---

*Our choice wasn't between a benign status quo and the
bloodshed of war. It was between war and a graver threat. Don't
let anyone tell you otherwise. Not our political opponents. And
certainly—and certainly not a disingenuous filmmaker.*

—John McCain

John McCain has achieved something rare in U.S. politics. He has
become a partisan figure who transcends partisanship, an individual
with whom both political parties clamor to associate. So much so, in
fact, that during the 2004 presidential election it was sometimes hard
to distinguish between each presidential candidates' television advertising, as warm images of McCain filled both. But this tug-of-war
battle to claim the reformist mantle of John McCain extended far
beyond mere political imagery. Behind the scenes, a grudge match of
inestimable importance had taken place between McCain's fellow
Vietnam combat veteran, John Kerry, and the man who had dashed
McCain's run for the White House in 2000, President George W. Bush.

But on August 30, 2004, McCain, a man whose body bears the scars
duty sometimes demands, assumed the rostrum at the Republican
National Convention in New York City and spoke the language of loyalty; he stood with his party and his president. And in the end, the Arizona senator's speech significantly aided in the president's reelection.

. . .

The thought had been swirling in Senator John Kerry's mind since August 2003. Still, to most observers the idea seemed like a long shot. The way Kerry saw it, however, there were at least four reasons why McCain might agree to switch parties and become his vice presidential running mate. First, it was no secret that the fallout surrounding McCain's bitter defeat during the 2000 Republican primaries had produced a thorny relationship with Bush. Second, while working together on Veteran's Affairs issues—even traveling to Hanoi together at one point—Kerry and McCain had grown close. Third, McCain's ubiquitous sobriquet, "Maverick," if now banal was firmly rooted in the senator's ethos and had become his trademark. And finally, McCain idolized Teddy Roosevelt, the Republican who had fled his party for an ill-fated presidential run as the candidate of his Bull Moose Party. Kerry hoped McCain might follow in the footsteps of his political hero and break from the GOP as well.

By March 2004, Kerry had clinched his party's nomination and henceforth made no less than six attempts to woo the Arizona senator. Kerry's determination was so complete that he extended an unprecedented offer: in exchange for joining the Democratic ticket, he would expand McCain's role as vice president to include secretary of Defense and control over U.S. foreign policy.

"You're out of your mind," McCain exclaimed. "I don't even know if it's constitutional, and it certainly wouldn't sell."

"G——dammit," Kerry yelled to an intermediary. "Don't you know what I offered him? Why the f—— didn't he take it? After what the Bush people did to him [during the 2000 Republican primaries]."[1]

But such is the way of the Maverick; he is equally adept at frustrating friend and foe alike. McCain is not unaware of the Janus-faced perceptions others have of him. On the one hand, he says a lot of people see him as "an independent-minded, well-intentioned public servant." On the other hand, he recognizes that "to others, I'm a self-styled, self-righteous, maverick pain in the ass."[2]

Either way, McCain's unpredictability was not conducive to Bush's reelection. With the election drawing near, the president and his chief strategist, Karl Rove, had grown increasingly concerned about which of these characterizations might prove most accurate. So Rove decided it was time to meet with John Weaver, one of McCain's advisers.

The two men met a few blocks from the White House at the Caribou Coffee Shop. They had at one time been close associates but had since cut ties following a past campaign squabble in Texas. Yet there, sitting together in the coffee shop, the two Republican strategists decided it was time to mend fences, and with them any remaining fissures between their candidates still left over from the 2000 election.

Some felt that McCain's decision to speak in prime time at the Republican National Convention in support of Bush was little more than a calculated attempt to position himself for a 2008 presidential run. But according to McCain, his primary reason for backing Bush remained his deep belief that the United States must win the War on Terror and that Bush was the right man for the job. Thus, the decision was made: McCain would speak at the Republican National Convention in New York City.

Mark Salter, the senator's longtime speechwriter and coauthor, helped craft McCain's convention speech. By now, he had become an expert at capturing his boss's cadence, something that came almost naturally. After all, it was a voice with which Salter was intimately familiar. His father, Corporal Pete Salter, had served in the navy during World War II and in the army during the Korean War. For his bravery during battle, Corporal Salter had been awarded the Silver Star and had the distinction of fighting alongside Congressional Medal of Honor recipient, Corporal Mitchell Red Cloud Jr. Like McCain, however, the senior Salter had always shied away from public discussions of his gallantry. "People write about how McCain is unnecessarily modest," the speechwriter says, "but it's perfectly consistent with the way my father talked about his war experience. The voice is perfectly consistent. The way [my dad] would talk real honestly about everything about the war except about what he did. . . . McCain's like that, too."[3]

Leading up to its unveiling on the opening night of the Republican

National Convention in Madison Square Garden, the speech had now entered its final phase of revisions. Because the major television networks had allotted only one hour of convention coverage for the evening, only McCain's and former New York mayor Rudy Giuliani's speeches would be televised. Planners had intended McCain to be the "warm-up act" to Giuliani, who was the keynote speaker. Some conservative party loyalists had expressed opposition to the absence of a more conservative voice; these criticisms proved to be short lived. According to Ramesh Ponnuru, the conservative senior editor at the *National Review*, McCain's speech helped create the most effective opening night of any political convention since 1992. To be sure, it would be one of the most memorable.

Standing on stage, McCain looked better than voters had seen him look in some time. Gone were the small bandages he sometimes wore on his face during his bout with melanoma. Ruddy of cheek, his suit lay taut on his shoulders, his tie a steely blue.

The speech began even and calm, like a gentle breeze. In true McCain fashion, his speech started with self-deprecation, which he then followed with a quote from Democratic president Franklin Delano Roosevelt. It was a move reminiscent of Ronald Reagan's 1980 acceptance speech, in which he also quoted FDR. In fact, McCain used the same FDR quote Reagan had during his 1964 televised speech in support of another Arizona politician, Barry Goldwater. "I begin with the words of a great American from the other party," McCain told his audience. "My purpose is not imitation, for I can't match his eloquence, but respect for the relevance in our time of his rousing summons to greatness of an earlier generation of Americans. . . . Franklin Delano Roosevelt accepted his party's nomination by observing: 'There is a mysterious cycle in human events. To some generations much is given. Of other generations much is expected. This generation of Americans has a rendezvous with destiny.'"

The audience responded with a polite volley of applause, the first in the speech. McCain then used his words to push back the hands of time and to focus the audience on the events that took place just blocks from where he stood. In so doing, McCain's rhetoric mirrored the president's. "It's a fight between right and wrong, good and evil," the senator said.

He then stoked the patriotic fires by reminding the audience of the surge of unity and strength Americans experienced following the horrors of 9/11. Given his reputation as someone who transcends party loyalties, McCain seemed a logical spokesperson to sound such a theme. "We must, whatever our disagreements, stick together in this great challenge of our time," he said. The bipartisan tenor continued. "My friends in the Democratic Party—and I'm fortunate to call many of them my friends—assure us they share the conviction that winning the war against terrorism is our government's most important obligation. I don't doubt their sincerity."

The line failed to generate applause, but that was hardly its purpose. McCain, whom polls have consistently shown draws support from voters of both political parties, wasn't speaking to those gathered in the convention hall, or even to the millions of Republicans throughout the country whose eyes were transfixed on their televisions. As the Republican's "leadoff hitter," the senator's remarks were designed to bolster his already strong ethos with those Democrats and Independents watching, with remote control in hand, who might still be teetering on the electoral fence.

McCain then spoke as only a man who has spent years as a prisoner of war can. "War is an awful business," he said. Then came the rhetorical pivot in his speech: "But there is no avoiding this war. We tried that, and our reluctance cost us dearly. . . . That is why I commend to my country the re-election of President Bush."

The audience erupted in raucous applause. McCain was almost a third of the way through the speech, and this was the first mention of the president by name. For those Republicans who had doubted the senator's party loyalty, it had come not a second too soon. He then reminded members of his party that he had spoken to them before: "Four years ago, in Philadelphia, I spoke of my confidence that President Bush . . ."

McCain then launched into an anaphora that served as a historical time line of President Bush's actions in the War on Terror. But more than that, his repeating refrains encapsulated the traits Americans so appreciated in their president in the wake of 9/11:

"He [Bush] promised . . ."

"He ordered . . ."

"He worked . . ."

"He encouraged . . ."

The audience punctuated each refrain by clapping, and with each line spoken, the applause grew louder and stronger in intensity. But no one, not even Senator McCain himself, was prepared for what would happen next.

Our choice wasn't between a benign status quo and the blood-shed of war. It was between war and a graver threat. Don't let anyone tell you otherwise. Not our political opponents. And certainly—and certainly not a disingenuous filmmaker who would have us believe . . ."

The roof lifted off the Garden as the audience booed.

Like fans doing the wave across a football stadium, a slow, rolling series of movements spread across the audience as people looked up at the press box and stabbed the air with their fingers. The next image television viewers saw was a quick cutaway to a live shot of *Fahrenheit 9/11* director and Kerry backer Michael Moore, who was inside the arena. Wearing a casual black zipper jacket, eyeglasses, and a red ball cap with the U.S. flag emblazoned on its face, the left-wing propagandist flashed a toothy grin back at McCain and the audience, took off his hat, and began pumping his fists in the air. McCain later said that he had no idea Moore was in the convention hall. Indeed, the senator seemed almost startled by the audience's unwillingness to settle back down. "Four more years! Four more years! Four more years!" they shouted.

The television cameras darted back to Moore, who was now making the letter *L*—a Generation-X hand gesture that stands for the word *loser*—with his right hand. It was not immediately clear to whom the filmmaker was referring.

The senator did his best to calm the rowdy crowd: "Please, please, my friends."

But like everyone watching, McCain felt the electricity surging through the Garden. It was a rare, unscripted instance of political theater played out before a live national audience. So the senator did what any good speaker would: he lived in the moment and hit his line a second time:

> *That line was so good, I'll use it again. Certainly not a disingenuous filmmaker . . .*

The audience erupted in deafening cheering and applause.

For a man who had spent his career *behind* the camera, Moore had suddenly found himself in an ironic reversal of roles. And it had happened on prime-time television.

Many wondered what the Kerry campaign was thinking when it allowed a lightning rod of controversy like Moore to attend the Republican National Convention. The answer: Annoyed that "[p]olitical conventions have become predictable rituals, four-day cheerleading sessions for both parties," *USA Today* granted Moore a press pass and space on its editorial page to give readers an "alternative perspective" on the GOP gathering in New York City. (After first hiring and then firing Ann Coulter, *USA Today* also asked conservative writer Jonah Goldberg to offer feedback on the Democratic National Convention in Boston). "I'm here to celebrate the fact that the Republicans only have a couple of months left," Moore smirked. "I'm here to celebrate the end of the Republican era."[4]

Whatever the reason for Moore being there, McCain's line had achieved two significant objectives. First, for those Republicans who had grown weary of McCain's maverick ways, slaying the liberal dragon responsible for *Fahrenheit 9/11*, a film despised by Republicans and fawned over by Bush-haters, effectively pardoned any and all past transgressions. Second, McCain had dangled bait in front of Moore, a master of self-promotion, that the filmmaker would lunge toward. Indeed, the very next day Moore's *USA Today* column centered entirely around McCain's line directed at him. The obligatory media frenzy and replaying of the now famous line quickly ensued.

In typical Michael Moore fashion, the filmmaker tried to spin the moment as having been positive. Not necessarily for the Democratic Party, but for his wallet: "The film's doing $120 million right now," Moore said. "When McCain mentions it, I have a chance to do $150 million."[5]

For someone who decries the evils of capitalism, it was an odd response. But more than that, Moore—and by extension the Kerry campaign—had revealed his fundamental lack of understanding of even rudimentary principles of political communications strategy and tactics. By reinforcing and reminding voters of Moore's close association with the Democratic Party and its presidential nominee, McCain had used the liberal filmmaker as the perfect foil to make the case that, like Moore, the Democratic Party and its nominee were simply too far outside the mainstream of U.S. politics. Best of all, the senator had done so without even mentioning the filmmaker by name.

Ironically, the decision to reference Moore in McCain's address may have been inspired by the Democratic National Convention one month prior in Boston. In a move that surprised both Republicans and Democrats alike, Moore had been invited as a guest of honor to sit in the presidential box with former president Jimmy Carter. Indeed, Moore's high visibility at both conventions only raised his perceived influence and stature within the Democratic Party. In addition, it put the terrorism issue front and center, since Moore's movie was, after all, about 9/11.

September 11 was also the subject of the rest of McCain's speech, one that proved surprisingly polemical. The senator advanced serious foreign policy arguments; namely, that Saddam Hussein's removal was justified and vital. "This president will not rest until America is stronger and safer still and this hateful iniquity is vanquished," McCain thundered (Hussein was captured by U.S. forces in December 2003). He then concluded in a crescendo of short sentences that brought the audience to their feet: "Keep your courage. Stick together. Stay strong. Do not yield. Do not flinch. Stand up. Stand up with our president and fight. We're Americans. We're Americans, and we'll never surrender. They will."

No sooner had the speech concluded than many of Moore's followers had logged on to liberal blogs to begin avenging McCain's jab at their patron saint. Blogs like News Hounds, a liberal blog hosted and maintained by Jim Gilliam, the producer of the anti–FOX News "documentary" *Outfoxed*, proved particularly venomous. One individual wrote: "Its [sic] about time you all realize that 'McRat' oh i [sic] mean McCain is not our friend. He is a snake in the grass. I wish the Cong [Vietcong] would have kept him. lol [laughing out loud]."[6]

But by focusing narrowly on McCain's reference to Moore, like most news organizations did, the full impact of McCain's rhetorical body blow against Kerry had gone unnoticed. Moreover, media failed to realize that McCain was the only messenger who could have delivered such an address.

For one, the Arizona senator's very presence at the convention was itself a devastating refutation of Kerry's overall campaign strategy. Beginning with his now infamous "I'm John Kerry and I'm reporting for duty" salute at the Democratic National Convention, the Kerry campaign had bet all its chips on convincing voters that their candidate was a rugged, manly patriot whose four-month stint in Vietnam proved he would not go soft in the War on Terror. The Swift Boat Veterans for Truth advertisements had raised serious questions in the minds of Vietnam veterans, many of whom had long believed Kerry's antiwar activities had been traitorous.

But others, McCain chief among them, felt that attacking the details surrounding Kerry's military medals missed the bigger picture—Kerry was the wrong man to fight and win the War on Terror. Indeed, if any of these voters had any doubts about who could best lead the battle against terrorism, they were all answered in McCain's speech. "After all," the logic went, "if John Kerry's first choice for vice president [McCain] wouldn't even support him, why should voters?"

What's more, "If one of America's most respected and well-known prisoners of war, and a man whom Kerry proudly called his close friend, was unwilling to join ranks with the Massachusetts senator, why should the general electorate?"

Interestingly, had Kerry not co-opted the McCain image and pursued him so aggressively as his vice presidential running mate, McCain's speech and twenty campaign appearances alongside President Bush might not have packed the same rhetorical punch. Nevertheless, McCain's speech—and the symbolism it generated—became a key component of the Bush victory and produced something rarely seen in the modern presidential era: a presidential convention marked by a moment of genuine, unscripted oratorical surprise.

It is, of course, impossible to know whether the outcome of the 2004 election would have been different had McCain abandoned the GOP ship and joined Kerry. But one thing *is* certain: from the start, Kerry wanted McCain, not John Edwards, as his running mate. That Kerry's top pick now stood solidly beside Bush, especially in light of their sometimes prickly relationship, was a fact the president's campaign wisely pounded home.

"We think it's important that people understand," said Bush campaign communications director Nicolle Devenish, "that this is a ticket of John Kerry and his second choice."[7]

Out on the campaign trail, the graying naval pilot, who had from 1967 to 1973 been a prisoner of war in Vietnam, dutifully joined his president to pump up the crowds and stand arm in arm with Bush. During these rallies, some reporters noted that it was sometimes hard to watch the senator struggle to hug people. Having endured countless beatings as a prisoner of war, McCain is no longer able to raise his arms much above his shoulders, thus making it awkward when attempting to hug others. But on the night of August 30, 2004, standing under the lights at Madison Square Garden, an American hero had embraced his party and president with a force far greater—his voice.

NOTES

Introduction   The Elephant Poachers: Leftist Academe and the Erasure of Republican Remembrance

The epigraph to this chapter is drawn from Milan Kundera, *The Book of Laughter and Forgetting* (New York: Penguin, 1981), 3.

1. Howard Kurtz, "College Faculties a Most Liberal Lot, Study Finds," *Washington Post*, March 29, 2005, C01. Also see Christopher F. Cardiff and Daniel B. Klein, "Faculty Partisan Affiliations in All Disciplines: A Voter Registration Study," *Critical Review* 17 (2005): 237–255.
2. Kurtz, "College Faculties a Most Liberal Lot, Study Finds."
3. See David Horowitz, *The Professors: The 101 Most Dangerous Academics in America* (Washington, DC: Regnery, 2006).
4. John Tierney, "Republicans Outnumbered in Academia, Studies Find," *New York Times*, November 18, 2004, www.nytimes.com/2004/11/18/education/18faculty.html?ex=1142226000&en=0f67bf488370f0e7&ei=5070.
5. Hunter Lewis, "Political Debate Sweeps Campus," *Herald-Sun*, February 12, 2004.
6. Mark Bauerlein, "Liberal Group Think Is Anti-Intellectual," *Chronicle of Higher Education*, November 12, 2004, http://chronicle.com/weekly/v51/i12/12b00601.htm.
7. American Council of Trustees and Alumni, "Intellectual Diversity," December 2005, www.goacta.org/publications/Reports/IntellectualDiversityFinal.pdf.

1   Abraham Lincoln: The First and Greatest

1. Doris Kearns Goodwin, *Team of Rivals: The Political Genius of Abraham Lincoln* (New York: Simon and Schuster, 2005), 48.

2. Garry Wills, *Lincoln at Gettysburg: The Words That Remade America* (New York: Simon and Schuster, 1992), 71.

3. Ronald C. White Jr., *The Eloquent President: A Portrait of Lincoln through His Words* (New York: Random House, 2005), 227–228.

4. Ibid.

5. David Herbert Donald, *Lincoln* (New York: Simon and Schuster, 1995), 460.

6. Ibid.

7. Edwin Black, "Gettysburg and Silence," *Quarterly Journal of Speech* 80 (1994): 21–36.

8. White, *Eloquent President*.

9. Ibid., 461.

10. Goodwin, *Team of Rivals*.

11. Donald, *Lincoln*.

12. Fred Stripp, "The Other Gettysburg Address," *Western Speech* 32 (1968): 20–21.

13. Wills, *Lincoln at Gettysburg*; David Zarefsky, "Rhetorical Interpretations of the American Civil War," *Quarterly Journal of Speech* 81 (1995): 108–138.

14. Goodwin, *Team of Rivals*, 586 (emphasis in original).

15. White, *Eloquent President*, 257.

16. Philip Van Doren Stern, *The Life and Writings of Abraham Lincoln* (New York: Modern Library, 2000), 789.

17. Ronald F. Reid, "Newspaper Response to the Gettysburg Address," *Quarterly Journal of Speech*.

18. Black, "Gettysburg and Silence," 27.

19. Eric Foner, *Freedom's Lawmakers: A Directory of Black Officeholders during Reconstruction* (Baton Rouge: Louisiana State University Press, 1996).

20. Allen W. Trelease, *White Terror: The Ku Klux Klan Conspiracy and Southern Reconstruction* (New York: Harper and Row, 1971), xlvii.

21. Goodwin, *Team of Rivals*, 697.

22. Ronald C. White Jr., *Lincoln's Greatest Speech: The Second Inaugural* (New York: Simon and Schuster, 2002).

23. William C. Harris, *Lincoln's Last Months* (Cambridge, MA: Belknap Press of Harvard University Press, 2004), 144.

24. Michael Leff, "Dimensions of Temporality in Lincoln's Second Inaugural," *Communication Reports* 1 (1988): 27.

25. Richard Nelson Current, *Speaking of Abraham Lincoln: The Man and His Meaning for Our Times* (Urbana: University of Illinois Press, 1983), 90.

26. Martha Solomon, "'With Firmness in the Right:' The Creation of Moral Hegemony in Lincoln's Second Inaugural," *Communication Reports* 1 (1988): 32–37.

27. White, *Eloquent President*, 296.

28. Harris, *Lincoln's Last Months*, 144.

29. Goodwin, *Team of Rivals*, 699.

30. Frederick Douglass, *Life and Times of Frederick Douglass* (New York: Scribner, 1962), 356–357.

31. Stern, *Life and Writings of Abraham Lincoln*, 842–843.

2 Theodore Roosevelt: The Rough-Riding Rhetorician

1. Candice Millard, *The River of Doubt: Theodore Roosevelt's Darkest Journey* (New York: Doubleday, 2006), 8.

2. Theodore Roosevelt, *The Rough Riders: An Autobiography* (New York: Library of America, 2004), 266.

3. Ibid, 271. Roosevelt wrote that "[t]he recollection of this experience gives me a keen sympathy with those who are trying in our public schools and elsewhere to remove the physical causes of deficiency in children, who are often unjustly blamed for being obstinate or unambitious, or mentally stupid."

4. Ibid., 280.

5. Ibid.

6. "Great American Speeches: Theodore Roosevelt," *Federal Observer* 6, no. 90 (January 28, 2006).

7. Patrick K. Dooley, "Public Policy and Philosophical Critique: The William James and Theodore Roosevelt Dialogue on Strenuousness," *Transactions of the Charles S. Peirce Society* 37 (2001): 170.

8. Roosevelt, *The Rough Riders*, 258.

9. Louis D. Rubin Jr., "TR," *Virginia Quarterly Review* (Winter 2005): 252.

10. Edmund Morris, *The Rise of Theodore Roosevelt* (New York: Coward, McCann and Geoghegan, 1979), 40.

11. Marvin Olasky, *The American Leadership Tradition: Moral Vision from Washington to Clinton* (New York: The Free Press, 1999), 177.

12. Allen Weinstein, "Theodore Roosevelt," in *"To the Best of My Ability": The American Presidents*, ed. James McPherson (New York: Dorling Kindersley, 2000), 181.

13. William A. Behl, "Theodore Roosevelt's Principles of Speech Preparation and Delivery," *Speech Monographs* 12 (1945): 112–122.

14. H. W. Brands, *T.R.: The Last Romantic* (New York: Basic Books, 1997), 91, 141.

15. Behl, "Theodore Roosevelt's Principles of Speech Preparation," 113.

16. Roosevelt, *The Rough Riders*, 276.

17. Behl, "Theodore Roosevelt's Principles of Speech Preparation," 113.

18. Mark Neuzil, "Hearst, Roosevelt, and the Muckrake Speech of 1906: A New Perspective," *Journalism and Mass Communication Quarterly* 73 (1996): 29–39; Herbert Croly, *The Promise of American Life* (Cambridge, MA: Belknap Press, 1965).

19. Edmund Morris, *Theodore Rex* (New York: Random House, 2001).

20. Neuzil, "Hearst, Roosevelt, and the Muckrake Speech of 1906," 33.
21. Ibid.
22. Neuzil, "Hearst, Roosevelt, and the Muckrake Speech of 1906," 34.
23. Lance Robinson, "Theodore Roosevelt (1858–1919)," in *American Conservatism: An Encyclopedia* (Wilmington, DE: Intercollegiate Studies Institute Books, 2006), 745.
24. Morris, *Theodore Rex*, 444.
25. Croly, *Promise of American Life*; Cynthia G. Emrich, et al., "Images in Words: Presidential Rhetoric, Charisma, and Greatness," *Administrative Science Quarterly* 46 (2001): 527–557.

3   William F. Buckley Jr.: American Conservatism Finds Its Spokesman in the Speech That Wasn't

1. William Rusher, *The Rise of the Right* (New York: William Morrow, 1984), 38; John Micklethwait and Adrian Wooldridge, *The Right Nation: Conservative Power in America* (New York: Penguin Press, 2004), 50.
2. William F. Buckley Jr., *Miles Gone By: A Literary Autobiography* (Washington, DC: Regnery, 2004).
3. "What NR Has Meant to Me," *National Review*, December 19, 2005, 64–70.
4. Ibid.
5. Jeff Jacoby, "There's No Stopping Bill Buckley," *Boston Globe*, July 1, 2004, www.boston.com/news/globe/editorial_opinion/oped/articles/2004/07/01/theres_no_stopping_bill_buckley/.
6. William F. Buckley Jr., *Gratitude: Reflections on What We Owe to Our Country* (New York: Random House, 1990), 155–156.
7. Buckley, *Miles Gone By*, 105.
8. William F. Buckley Jr., *God and Man at Yale: The Superstitions of "Academic Freedom"* (Washington, DC: Regnery, 1986), 134.
9. Ibid., 129.
10. Ibid., 130.
11. Buckley, *Miles Gone By*, 106.

4   Dwight D. Eisenhower: Strategic Speechifying

1. Fred I. Greenstein, *The Hidden-Hand Presidency: Eisenhower as Leader* (New York: Basic Books, 1982).
2. Geoffrey Perret, *Eisenhower* (New York: Random House, 1999), 287.
3. Martin J. Medhurst, "Eisenhower's Atoms for Peace Speech: A Case Study in the Strategic Use of Language," *Communication Monographs* 54 (1987): 204–221.
4. Ira Chernus, *Eisenhower's Atoms for Peace* (College Station: Texas A&M University Press, 2002).

5. Ibid., 10.
6. Robert H. Ferrell, *The Eisenhower Diaries* (New York: Norton, 1981), 262.
7. Dwight D. Eisenhower, *The White House Years: Mandate for Change, 1953–1956* (New York: Doubleday, 1963), 254.
8. Medhurst, "Eisenhower's Atoms for Peace Speech," 221.
9. Perret, *Eisenhower*, 550; *Public Papers of the President of the United States: Eisenhower, 1957* (Washington, DC: U.S. Government Printing Office, 1958), 546–555.
10. It is interesting to note that Barry Goldwater would later echo this very sentiment with regard to the Civil Rights Act of 1964, yet his message would be received and reported in the mainstream media in an entirely different tone and context. Steven R. Goldzwig and George N. Dionisopoulos, "Crisis at Little Rock: Eisenhower, History, and Mediated Political Realities," in *Eisenhower's War of Words: Rhetoric and Leadership*, ed. Martin J. Medhurst (Lansing: Michigan State University Press, 1994), 202; "The President's News Conference of September 3, 1957," *Public Papers: 1957*, 640, 646.
11. Goldzwig and Dionisopoulos, "Crisis at Little Rock," 199; "The News of the Week in Review: Up to Faubus," *New York Times*, September 15, 1957, 4, E1.
12. Ibid., 196.
13. Perret, *Eisenhower*, 551
14. Ibid.
15. Goldzwig and Dionisopoulos, "Crisis at Little Rock," 206; Stephen E. Ambrose, *Eisenhower: The President* (New York: Simon and Schuster, 1984), 418.
16. Perret, *Eisenhower*, 552
17. Ibid.
18. Goldzwig and Dionisopoulos, "Crisis at Little Rock," 215.

5 Everett Dirksen: The Speech That Made the Civil Rights Act of 1964 Possible

1. Tony Brown, *Black Lies, White Lies* (New York: Quill William Morrow, 1995), 235.
2. U.S. Senator Robert C. Byrd, http://byrd.senate.gov/biography/senators/senators.html
3. Ibid.
4. Michelle Malkin, "Democratic Sen. Robert Byrd, Ex-Klansman," *Capitalism*, March 8, 2001, www.capmag.com/article.asp?ID=383.
5. Eric Pianin, "A Senator's Shame," *Washington Post*, June 19, 2005, A01.
6. Malkin, "Democratic Sen. Robert Byrd."
7. Arthur M. Schlesinger Jr., *A Thousand Days: John F. Kennedy in the White House* (Boston: Houghton Mifflin, 1965), 971.

8. Schlesinger, *Thousand Days*, 969.

9. Robert A. Caro, *Master of the Senate: The Years of Lyndon Johnson* (New York: Alfred A. Knopf, 2002), xv.

10. Robert Parker, *Capitol Hill in Black and White* (New York: Dodd Mead, 1986), v, vi, 16, 23.

11. Dirksen Center, "E. Dirksen Notebook, n.d.," www.congresslink.org/print_ basics_histmats_civilrights64_doc3.htm.

12. U.S. Senate, "Civil Rights Filibuster Ended," June 10, 1964, www.senate .gov/artandhistory/history/minute/Civil_Rights_Filibuster_Ended.htm.

13. Robert Mann, *The Walls of Jericho: Lyndon Johnson, Hubert Humphrey, Richard Russell, and the Struggle for Civil Rights* (San Francisco: Harcourt Brace, 1996), 409.

14. "The Covenant," *Time*, June 19, 1964; Everett McKinley Dirksen, *The Education of a Senator* (Urbana: University of Illinois Press, 1998).

15. "The Covenant."

16. "Everett McKinley Dirksen's Finest Hour: June 10, 1964," *Peoria Journal Star*, June 10, 2004.

17. Mann, *Walls of Jericho*, 395.

18. Michael Beschloss, Landon lecture, Kansas State University, March 6, 2003.

19. Dirksen Center, "E. Dirksen Notebook."

20. Dirksen, *Education of a Senator*, xxxiii.

21. Mann, *Walls of Jericho*, 411.

22. "The Covenant."

23. John G. Stewart, "The Civil Rights Act of 1964: Tactics II," in *The Civil Rights Act of 1964: The Passage of the Law That Ended Racial Segregation*, ed. Robert D. Loevy (Albany: State University of New York Press, 1997), 296–297.

24. Nicholas Lehmann, "On the Way with L.B.J," *New York Times*, July 21, 1991.

25. Roy Wilkins letter to Everett Dirksen, June 12, 1964. Available at the Dirksen Center, www.congresslink.org/civil/cr19.gif.

26. "The Covenant."

27. "Thanks to Dirksen," *Chicago Daily News*, June 5, 1964.

6 Barry Goldwater: "You Know He's Right"

1. Lloyd G. Daugherty, "Barry Goldwater Spawned a Revolution," *Human Events*, July 24, 1998.

2. Sam Tanenhaus, "The GOP, or Goldwater's Old Party," *New Republic*, June 11, 2001, 8.

3. John McCain, "Eulogy of Barry Goldwater," *Essential Speeches*, June 3, 1998, 1.

4. Lee Edwards, "The Unforgettable Candidate," *National Review*, July 6, 1998, 26.

5. "Barry Goldwater and 'Old Conservatism,'" *Church & State*, July–August 1998, 14.

6. Michael J. Gerson and Mike Tharp, "Mr. Right," *U.S. News & World Report*, June 8, 1998, 16.

7. Richard Brookhiser, "Youth Movement," *National Review*, July 6, 1998, 31; John C. Hammerback, "Barry Goldwater's Rhetoric of Rugged Individualism," *Quarterly Journal of Speech* 58 (1972): 175–184.

8. Barry Goldwater, *The Conscience of a Conservative* (Washington, DC: Regnery, 1994).

9. Edwards, "Unforgettable Candidate"; Ernest J. Wrage, "The Little World of Barry Goldwater," *Western Speech* (1963): 210.

10. Edwards, "Unforgettable Candidate," 28.

11. Ibid.

12. Ibid.

13. Glenn Garvin, "He Was Right," *Reason*, March 2002, 6.

14. William Rentschler, "Barry Goldwater: Icon of Political Integrity," *USA Today Magazine*, March 2000, 70.

15. Robert Mann, *The Walls of Jericho: Lyndon Johnson, Hubert Humphrey, Richard Russell, and the Struggle for Civil Rights* (San Diego: Harvest, 1996), 430.

16. Gerson and Tharp, "Mr. Right."

17. Linda Feldmann, "Republicans Step Up Efforts to Bring Blacks into the Party," *Christian Science Monitor*, October 17, 2005, www.csmonitor.com/2005/1017/p01s03-uspo.html.

18. Martin Luther King Jr., *The Autobiography of Martin Luther King Jr.*, ed. Clayborne Carson (New York: Warner Books, 1998), 247.

19. Garvin, "He Was Right," 6.

20. Edwards, "Unforgettable Candidate," 36.

21. John Micklethwait and Adrian Wooldridge, *The Right Nation: Conservative Power in America* (New York: Penguin Press, 2004), 60.

22. Henry Jaffe, "Goldwater's Famous 'Gaffe,'" *National Review*, August 10, 1984, 36.

23. Edwards, "Unforgettable Candidate," 36.

24. Hammerback, "Barry Goldwater's Rhetoric of Rugged Individualism."

25. Also see Thomas Sowell, *A Conflict of Visions: Ideological Origins of Political Struggles* (New York: Basic Books, 2002).

26. Edwards, "Unforgettable Candidate," 36.

27. Rentschler, "Barry Goldwater," 73.

7 Richard M. Nixon: The Beginning of the End

1. Herbert S. Parmet, *Richard Nixon and His America* (New York: Konecky and Konecky, 1990).

2. Celeste Michelle Condit, "Nixon's 'Fund': Time as Ideological Resource in the 'Checkers' Speech," in *Texts in Context: Critical Dialogues on Significant Episodes in American Political Rhetoric*, ed. Michael C. Leff and Fred J. Kauffeld (David, CA: Hermagoras Press, 1989), 220.

3. Parmet, *Richard Nixon and His America*, 245.

4. Ibid.

5. Karlyn Kohrs Campbell and Kathleen Hall Jamieson, *Deeds Done in Words: Presidential Rhetoric and the Genres of Governance* (Chicago: University of Chicago Press, 1990), 129–130.

6. "Checkers" wasn't the only time Nixon used personal storytelling and biographical information to create an image that voters could relate to. As Kathleen Hall Jamieson notes, Nixon later used the technique brilliantly in his 1968 Republican National Convention acceptance speech, wherein he references having had "[a] father who had to go to work before he finished the sixth grade, sacrificed everything he had so that his sons could go to college. A gentle, Quaker mother, with a passionate concern for peace." Kathleen Hall Jamieson, *Eloquence in an Electronic Age: The Transformation of Political Speechmaking* (New York: Oxford University Pres, 1988), 137.

7. Thomas B. Farrell, "The Carnival as Confessional: Re-reading the Figurative Dimension in Nixon's 'Checkers' Speech," in *Texts in Context: Critical Dialogues on Significant Episodes in American Political Rhetoric*, ed. by Michael C. Leff and Fred J. Kauffeld (David, CA: Hermagoras Press, 1989), 250.

8. Elizabeth Burmiller, "It's a Loyal Ally but May Dig Up Trouble," *New York Times*, August 22, 1996, B1.

9. Parmet, *Richard Nixon and His America*, 246.

10. Ibid.

11. Condit, "Nixon's 'Fund,'" 239.

12. During the Clinton-Lewinsky scandal in 1998, for example, an article by Caryn James appeared in the August 18 *New York Times* with the title: WILL CLINTON'S SPEECH DO FOR HIM WHAT CHECKERS DID FOR NIXON?

13. Parmet, *Richard Nixon and His America*, 238.

8   Gerald R. Ford: "Our Long National Nightmare Is Over"

1. Craig R. Smith, "Richard M. Nixon and Gerald R. Ford: Lessons on Speechwriting," in *Presidential Speechwriting: From the New Deal to the Reagan Revolution and Beyond*, ed. Kurt Ritter and Martin J. Medhurst (College Station: Texas A&M University Press, 2003), 153.

2. Ibid., 140.

3. Fred I. Greenstein, *The Presidential Leadership Difference: Leadership Style from FDR to Clinton* (New York: The Free Press, 2000), 112.

4. Ibid., 113.
5. Ibid.
6. Steven Hayward, *The Age of Reagan: The Fall of the Old Liberal Order*, 1964–1980 (New York: Forum Prima, 2001), 396.

9 Ronald Reagan: A Shining Speaker on a Hill

1. Paul Kengor, *God and Ronald Reagan: A Spiritual Life* (New York: ReganBooks, 2004), 74.
2. Ibid, 235.
3. William Ker Muir Jr., *Bully Pulpit: The Presidential Leadership of Ronald Reagan* (San Francisco, CA: Institute for Contemporary Studies Press, 1992), 77.
4. Ibid.
5. Kengor, *God and Ronald Reagan*, 238.
6. Lou Cannon, *President Reagan: The Role of a Lifetime* (New York: Public Affairs, 2000), 274. For the definitive history of Reagan's lifelong battle against Communism, see Peter Schweizer, *Reagan's War: The Epic Story of His Forty-Year Struggle and Final Triumph over Communism* (New York: Doubleday, 2002).
7. Dick Wirthlin and Wynton C. Hall, *The Greatest Communicator: What Ronald Reagan Taught Me about Politics, Leadership, and Life* (Hoboken, NJ: John Wiley & Sons, 2004), 96.
8. Peter Robinson, *How Ronald Reagan Changed My Life* (New York: ReganBooks, 2003), 92.
9. Peggy Noonan, *When Character Was King: A Story of Ronald Reagan* (New York: Penguin Books, 2001), 214.
10. Wirthlin and Hall, *Greatest Communicator*, 180.
11. Randall L. Bytwerk, "Ronald Reagan's Eulogy of the *Challenger*," in *Great Speeches for Criticism and Analysis*, ed. Lloyd Rohler and Roger Cook (Greenwood, IN: Alistair Press, 1988), 311–319.
12. Mary E. Stuckey, *Slipping the Surly Bonds: Reagan's* Challenger *Address* (College Station: Texas A&M University Press, 2006), 9.
13. Wirthlin and Hall, *Greatest Communicator*, 181.
14. Peggy Noonan, *What I Saw at the Revolution: A Political Life in the Reagan Era* (New York: Ivy Books, 1990), 262.
15. Ibid., 264.
16. Kiron K. Skinner, Annelise Anderson, and Martin Anderson, *Reagan: A Life in Letters* (New York: The Free Press, 2003), 567.
17. Stuckey, *Slipping the Surly Bonds*, 63.
18. Bytwerk, "Ronald Reagan's Eulogy of the *Challenger*," 318; *U.S. News & World Report*, February 19, 1986, 21.
19. Stuckey, *Slipping the Surly Bonds*, 62–63.

20. Noonan, *What I Saw at the Revolution*, 266.

21. Ibid., 267.

22. Edmund Morris, *Dutch: A Memoir of Ronald Reagan* (New York: Modern Library, 1999), 586.

23. Richard V. Allen, "The Man Who Won the Cold War," *Hoover Digest*, no. 1 (2000), www.hooverdigest.org/001/allen.html; this essay also appears in the fabulous treatise on the subject, Peter Schweizer, *The Fall of the Berlin Wall: Reassessing the Causes and Consequences of the End of the Cold War* (Stanford, CA: Hoover Institution Press, 2000).

24. Schweizer, *Reagan's War*, 12–13.

25. Ibid., 183.

26. Ronald Reagan, *An American Life: The Autobiography* (New York: Simon and Schuster, 1990), 680.

27. Robinson, *How Ronald Reagan Changed My Life*, 97–98.

28. Wirthlin and Hall, *Greatest Communicator*, 196.

29. Reagan, *American Life*, 680–681.

30. In his much-maligned biography of Reagan, Edmund Morris mocks the event and speech as having been "too staged, the crowd too small and well-primed, to make for genuine drama. . . . What a rhetorical opportunity missed. According to Morris, the president would have been much better served had he instead read passages of a Robert Frost poem. Morris, *Dutch*, 624–625.

31. Schweizer, *Reagan's War*, 38–39.

32. Robinson, *How Ronald Reagan Changed My Life*, 107.

33. Kengor, *God and Ronald Reagan*, 282.

34. Kurt Ritter and David Henry, *Ronald Reagan: The Great Communicator* (New York: Greenwood Press, 1992).

35. F. A. Hayek, *The Fatal Conceit: The Errors of Socialism*, ed. W. W. Bartley III (Chicago: University of Chicago Press, 1988).

10   Newt Gingrich: The Revolutionary Speaker

1. Brad Miner, *The Concise Conservative Encyclopedia* (New York: The Free Press, 1996), 90–91.

2. Gail Sheehy, "The Inner Quest of Newt Gingrich," *Vanity Fair*, September 1995, www.pbs.org/wgbh/pages/frontline/newt/vanityfair1.html.

3. Newt Gingrich, *To Renew America* (New York: HarperCollins, 1995), 118.

4. Ibid., 118–119.

5. David Frum, *Dead Right* (New York: Basic Books, 1994).

6. Newt Gingrich, *Winning the Future: A 21st Century Contract with America* (Washington, DC: Regnery, 2005), xix.

7. John Micklethwait and Adrian Wooldridge, *The Right Nation: Conservative Power in the Nation* (New York: Penguin Press, 2004); Ed Gillespie and Bob Schellhas, *Contract with America: The Bold Plan by Rep. Newt Gingrich, Rep. Dick*

Armey and the House Republicans to Change the Nation (New York: Times Books, 1994).

8. Gingrich, *To Renew America*, 43.

9. Ibid., 21.

10. For the continuing legacy of these efforts, see Major Garrett, *The Enduring Revolution: How the Contract with America Continues to Shape the Nation* (New York: Crown Forum, 2005).

11. Gingrich, *Winning the Future*, xix.

12. Ibid., xviii

13. David Maraniss and Michael Weisskopf, *"Tell Newt to Shut Up!"* (New York: Touchstone, 1996).

14. Joe Klein, "Why Newt Is So Much Fun to Watch," *Time*, April 16, 2006.

11   George W. Bush: His Mission and His Moment

1. David Zarefsky, "George W. Bush Discovers Rhetoric: September 20, 2001, and the U.S. Response to Terrorism," in *The Ethos of Rhetoric*, ed. Michael J. Hyde (Columbia: University of South Carolina Press, 2004), 152.

2. Peggy Noonan, "God Is Back," *Wall Street Journal*, September 28, 2001. Republished in Peggy Noonan, *A Heart, a Cross, and a Flag* (New York: Wall Street Journal Books, 2003), 16.

3. Bob Woodward, *Bush at War* (New York: Simon and Schuster, 2002), 15.

4. Peter Schweizer and Rochelle Schweizer, *The Bushes: Portrait of a Dynasty* (New York: Doubleday, 2004), 516.

5. Dan Balz and Bob Woodward, "A Presidency Defined in One Speech," *Washington Post*, February 2, 2002, A01.

6. Karen Hughes, *Ten Minutes from Normal* (New York: Viking, 2004), 257.

7. Frank Bruni, the *New York Times* columnist who wrote an early Bush biography of sorts based on his coverage of the 2000 Bush campaign, had this to say about Bush's use of the term *evildoers:* "Bush ceaselessly referred to the terrorists and those who harbored them as 'evildoers' and to Osama bin Laden as 'the evil one,' terms that sounded alternately archaic and apocalyptic and cast the country's struggle as one of righteousness versus immorality, the servants of virtue versus Beelzebub himself. During his address to Congress [September 20, 2001], Bush interpreted this crossroads in America's history in grand, emphatic and even Manichaean terms that suggested the influence of his faith." Frank Bruni, *Ambling into History* (New York: HarperCollins, 2002), 257.

8. Schweizer and Schweizer, *Bushes*, 517.

9. Hughes, *Ten Minutes from Normal*, 256–257.

10. Carl M. Cannon, "Soul of a Conservative," *National Journal*, May 14, 2005.

11. David Frum, *The Right Man: The Surprise Presidency of George W. Bush* (New York: Random House, 2003), 25.

12. Ibid.

13. Jeffrey Goldberg, "The Believer," *New Yorker*, February 13, 2006, www.newyorker.com/printables/fac7/060213fa_fact/.

14. Karen Hughes, *Ten Minutes from Normal*, 258–259.

15. Tony Carnes, "Bush's Defining Moment," *Christianity Today* 45 (2001): 38–42.

16. Alan Cooperman, "Bush's References to God Defended by Speechwriter," *Washington Post*, December 12, 2004, A06.

17. Goldberg, "Believer."

18. Carnes, "Bush's Defining Moment," 40.

19. Balz and Woodward, "Presidency Defined in One Speech."

20. Hughes, *Ten Minutes from Normal*, 258.

21. Julia Keller, "After the Attack, Postmodernism Loses Its Glib Grip," *Chicago Tribune*, September 27, 2001.

22. Michael Gerson, "The Danger for America Is Not Theocracy," (lecture, Ethics and Public Policy Center, Pier House, Key West, Florida, December 2004).

23. Kenneth Burke, *A Rhetoric of Motives* (Berkeley: University of California Press, 1984), 22.

24. Hughes, *Ten Minutes from Normal*.

25. William Schneider, "A Generational Call to Arms," *National Journal*, September 29, 2001, 304.

26. The White House, www.whitehouse.gov/march11/message11.html.

27. The White House, www.whitehouse.gov/march11/message10.html.

28. Goldberg, "Believer."

29. Ibid.

12   John McCain: The Maverick and His Message

1. *Newsweek*, November 15, 2004, 78.

2. John McCain, *Worth the Fighting For: The Education of an American Maverick and the Heroes Who Inspired Him* (New York: Random House, 2003), xvii.

3. Jake Tapper, "Mark Salter: The Voice of Sen. John McCain," *Salon*, October 12, 1999, http://archive.salon.com/news/feature/1999/10/12.

4. John Nichols, "McCain v. Moore," *Nation*, August 31, 2004; the Online Beat, www.thenation.com/blogs/thebeat?pid-1733.

5. Mark Leibovich and Paul Farhi, "Michael Moore Joins the Press—and Gets Some," *Washington Post*, August 31, 2004, C01.

6. New Hounds, www.newshounds.us/2004/08/31/mccains_michael_moore_comment.php.

7. Richard W. Stevenson and Jim Rutenberg, "Bush Campaign Sees an Opportunity for Attack in Kerry's Overture to McCain," *New York Times*, July 6, 2004, A17.

INDEX

Nancy (mother), 14
plain oratory style of, 21
rhetorical devices of, 17–20, 23, 28, 31–35
Sarah (sister), 14
slavery and, 26, 27, 30–34, 152
Thomas (brother and uncle), 14
Willie (son), 15
See also Gettysburg Address; Second
    Inaugural Address
Little Rock integration riots, 85–90
Little Rock speech, text of, 87–89
Losing Ground (Murray), 180

Magee, John Gillespie, 162
Magnet, Myron, 180
male responsibility, 41, 45
man with a muck-rake speech (Roosevelt)
    Pilgrim's Progress cited in, 54, 56
    response to, 57
    text of, 56–57
    yellow journalism and, 53–55
Mansfield, Mike, 97, 107
marriage, in Roosevelt's time, 45
Marshall, Thurgood, 106
Marxist ideology, 7, 72
McCain, John, 41, 211–20
    Roosevelt's ideals and, 41
McConnell, John, 193, 194, 195
McFarlane, Bud, 160
McKinley, William, 44, 49
Meade, Gordon, 16
Medhurst, Martin J., 77, 82
media
    Contract with America and, 177, 185
    Donaldson, 148
    "evil empire" speech criticized by, 155
    Gettysburg Address and, 22–23
    liberal bias of, 53, 54–57
    yellow journalism and, 53–54, 57
metaphors, 17–18, 20, 23, 54, 168, 170, 171
military strength
    buildups during peacetime, 47–48
    Reagan and, 44, 48, 148, 152, 153–55, 167
    as Republican ideal, 9, 44, 48, 152, 167
    restraint in domestic use of, 85, 86, 87–89
    Roosevelt and, 43–44, 46–49
Mill, John Stuart, 5
Millard, Candice, 39
Moore, Michael, 198, 216–20

moral certainty, 148, 153–54
moral choice making, 8
moral equivalency, 192, 199
moral freedom, 148, 151
moral relativism, 66
Morris, Edmund, 44, 57
mudslinging, 55
Muir, William Ker Jr., 148
Murray, Charles, 180
Muslims, 199–200

National Aeronautics and Space Adminis-
    tration (NASA), 157, 160, 161
National Association for the Advancement of
    Colored People (NAACP), 100, 107–8
national defense. *See* military strength
National Endowment for the Humanities,
    6
National Review, 62–63, 71
National Security Council, 160, 165
Nevitte, Niel, 4
New Republic, 53
New York Journal, 54
Nixon, Pat, 129, 133
Nixon, Richard
    Checkers speech, 129–36
    pardon of, 139, 141, 143
    resignation of, 136
    as vice presidential candidate, 127, 128,
        134
    Watergate scandal and, 136
Noonan, Peggy, 158, 160, 162, 190
nuclear freeze, 148, 152, 153–55

Olasky, Marvin, 45, 180, 182–83
O'Neill, Tip, 162, 175
Oppenheimer Report, 77

parental notification of abortion, 150–51,
    152
Parker, Robert, 96
partisanship and policy, 8–9
Pataki, George, 201–2
peace as a weapon, 77, 78, 80, 81–83
peace through strength policy, 152, 167
Peloponnesian War, 19
Pentagon terrorist attack, 191
Pericles's Funeral Oration, 19
Phillips, David Graham, 54, 55